The

LITTLE BOOK

of

CLOUD
COMPUTING

HARRY KATZAN JR.

THE LITTLE BOOK OF CLOUD COMPUTING

iUniverse books may be ordered through booksellers or by contacting:

iUniverse
1663 Liberty Drive
Bloomington, IN 47403
www.iuniverse.com
844-349-9409

ISBN: 978-1-6632-4040-8 (sc)
ISBN: 978-1-6632-4042-2 (hc)
ISBN: 978-1-6632-4041-5 (e)

Library of Congress Control Number: 2022909908

Print information available on the last page.

iUniverse rev. date: 05/26/2022

To Margaret, as always

PREFACE

This book is a collection of short chapters on three important topics: Cloud computing, privacy, and identity. The topics are related but have a separate focus.

Cloud computing is a model for providing on-demand access to computing service via the Internet. The Internet is the connection between a client and a service located somewhere in cyberspace, as compared to having computer applications residing on an "on premises" computer. Cloud computing eliminates two problems in providing computer service: the upfront costs of acquiring computational resources and the time delay of building and deploying software applications. The technology is not without a downside, which, in this case, is the privacy of business and personal information that links the constituent topics together.

The chapters are intended to be read separately resulting in a minor amount of definitional material being repeated. The reader is able to comfortably read the papers on a topic of interest and disregard the remainder.

The first chapter entitled **The Privacy of Cloud Computing** sets the stage for the compendium by establishing the link between cloud computing and privacy. It contains good reference material on the subject matter.

The second chapter paper entitled **Identity as a Service** covers the complex topic of personal identity, which has been an important for philosophers and scientists.

The third chapter entitled **Identity Analytics and Belief Structures** continues with the subject of identity by using mathematical techniques for dealing with identity management and categorizing subjects.

The fourth chapter entitled **Compatibility Relations in Identity Analysis** continues with the mathematical treatment of identity by relating constituent namespaces.

The fifth chapter entitled **Conspectus of Cloud Computing** introduces the business value of cloud computing and provides a context for subsequent studies of the subject.

The sixth chapter entitled **Cloud Computing Economics: Democratization and Monetization of Services** gives information on the monetization and democratization of cloud computing services.

The seventh chapter entitled **Ontological View of Cloud Computing** gives a more formal treatment of cloud computing with an emphasis on the language elements of cloud computing.

The eighth chapter entitled **Privacy as a Service** covers why privacy is so important in everyday life and why society should provide "privacy as a service."

The ninth chapter, entitled **Liberty, Freedom, and Rights,** covers why it is necessary to view privacy and identity in a larger context of liberty, freedom, and rights. An individual who is free can select goals, appropriate alternatives, and is not restricted in thought or action by the will or presence of another person. The paper covers the classic struggle between liberty and authority.

The tenth and last chapter, entitled **Global Data Regulation,** covers the ubiquitous use of computers and communications technology, and the transfer of data across worldwide boundaries, in the context of social, economic, and political conditions related to the transborder flow of personal information.

The Appendix gives the United States Privacy Act, and the addendum provides a combined list of references.

It is hoped that this little book will give some exposure to the topics and generate interest in an important facet of modern computing.

HARRY KATZAN, JR.

CONTENTS

Cloud computing is a model for providing on-demand access to computing service via the Internet. In this instance, the Internet is the transport mechanism between a client and a server located somewhere in cyberspace, as compared to having computer applications residing on an "on premises" computer. Adoption of cloud computing practically eliminates two ongoing problems in IT service provisioning: the upfront costs of acquiring computational resources and the time delay of building and deploying software applications. The technology is not without a downside, which in this case is the privacy of business and personal information. This paper provides a conspectus of the major issues in cloud computing privacy and should be regarded as an introductory paper on this important topic.

Identity service is an important subject in information systems in general and cloud computing in particular. Normally associated with digital security and privacy, the scope of identity is much greater and affects most aspects of everyday life. Related subjects are behavioral tracking, personal-identifiable information (PII), privacy data relevance, data repurposing, and identity theft. Cloud computing is currently portrayed as a model for providing on-demand access to computing service via the Internet and also serves as a focus for modern security and privacy concerns. Identity service is an admixture of the major issues in the privacy and security of individual rights in a complex informational environment. This is a working paper on this important subject.

Personal identity is an important topic in information systems in general and data analytics in particular. Normally associated with digital security and privacy, the scope of identity is much greater and affects most aspects of everyday life. Related subjects are behavioral tracking, personal-identifiable information (PII), privacy data relevance, data repurposing, identity theft, and homeland security. The purpose of this paper is to establish a context for using analytics to combine evidence to categorize certain subjects based on belief structures.

Methods for categorizing certain subjects, based on belief structures, are an important aspect of modern society. In an accompanying paper, we present a method for combining belief, attributable to diverse knowledge sources, in order to obtain a measure of group membership. The scope of group identity is much greater than digital security and affects other societal endeavors. In this paper, we are going to propose methods for propagating belief through a complex network of belief assessments. The methods are known as compatibility relations. The referenced paper is *Identity Analytics and Belief Structures*, included in this compendium.

Cloud computing is a technique for supplying computer facilities and providing access to software via the Internet. Cloud computing represents a contextual shift in how computers are provisioned and accessed. One of the defining characteristics of cloud software service is the transfer of control from the client domain to the service provider. Another is that the client benefits from economy of scale on the part of the provider. Cloud computing is particularly attractive to small and medium-sized organizations, because it represents a lower total cost of ownership (TCO) than alternative modalities.

Cloud computing is a modality for providing computer services via the Internet, by incorporating ubiquitous access through a web browser for the execution of single-function applications, such as those available as office suites, and comprehensive enterprise line-of-business applications pieced together from components residing in varying Internet locations. This paper covers the democratization and monetization of software services and uses cloud computing as the primary delivery vehicle. Cloud computing represents a contextual shift in how computers are provisioned and accessed. There is opportunity and value in cloud computing for providers, ISVs, and customers. The subject is covered from an economic perspective for each of the groups.

Cloud computing is an architecture for providing computing service via the Internet. Use of the term "cloud" is a metaphor for the representation of the Internet used in most systems diagrams. In this case, the Internet is the transport mechanism between a client and a server located somewhere in cyberspace, as compared to having computer applications residing on an "on premises" computer. Adoption of cloud computing practically eliminates two ongoing problems in IT service provisioning: the upfront costs of acquiring computational resources and the time delay of building and deploying software applications. This paper gives an ontological view of the subject in order to serve as a point of reference in the discipline and to facilitate ongoing technical development.

Many persons feel that there is more intrusion into our everyday lives than we want, expect, and deserve. Through organization, such as government, education, and business, coupled with technology, such as the Internet, cloud computing, information systems, information brokers, and social networking systems, it would seem that any hope we have for a semblance of personal privacy is gone. On the other hand, privacy advocates foster the belief that privacy is a service that should be engendered by society as a whole and individuals in particular. This paper covers privacy-as-a-service as it relates to biometrics, video surveillance, data profiling, behavioral tracking, and Internet records.

Freedom is a social concept that refers to the relationship among individuals in an interpersonal environment. An individual who is free can select goals, appropriate alternatives, and is not restricted in thought or action by the will or presence of another person. Important considerations are conditions under which actions would be performed and the means by which they are performed. A key word in the concept of freedom is coercion. In general, freedom from coercion is embodied in two concepts: negative freedom and positive freedom. This paper provides an essential review of liberty, freedom, and rights.

Because of the ubiquitous use of computers and communications technology, there are no boundaries to the worldwide flow of data. The professional, scientific, and economic value of a modern world based on Internet technology is enormous. There are differing views, however, on the international flow of personal data that have resulted in various laws on data regulation. This paper gives a brief overview of this important topic.

1

THE PRIVACY OF CLOUD COMPUTING

INTRODUCTION

It seems as though most computer users would like privacy and information security while having convenient access to interlinked computing services both on-premises and in the cloud. In this instance, the cloud is a metaphor for the Internet, which can be used as the delivery vehicle for computing services and the storage of information. Advocates of cloud computing are faced with two major problems, that is, in addition to the usual problem of transferring one's resources from one operational environment to another. The first of the major problems is the ongoing feeling that we are experiencing the "déjà vu all over again" syndrome. Many of us have gone through an avalanche of new technological advances intended as solutions to our administrative and operational problems – at least, the ones involving management and information systems. Some of the technical innovations we have experienced include scalable mainframe computers, advanced operating systems, time sharing, client/ server, online systems, mini computers, personal computers, artificial intelligence, hand-held computers, the Internet and the World Wide Web, mobile computers, social networking, and by the time this paper is published, there will no doubt be several more entries to add to the list. So one has reason to be skeptical of someone writing that cloud computing is worthy of serious attention. Of course, we think it is, for obvious reasons.

The second major issue is privacy, and it stems from the fact that with cloud computing, data and programs are stored off-premises and managed by a service provider. When a third party gets a hold of your data, who knows what is going to happen to it. Many proponents of cloud computing conveniently characterize it as analogous to the electric utility. The basic idea is that the private generators of the twentieth century were replaced by the electricity grids of today without undue concern. It is easy to imagine, however, that the measurement of electricity usage would have been of concern to some people in the early 1900s. Although similar in some respects, cloud computing is different in one important way. The cloud will typically handle information, which is the basic unit of exchange, about which security and privacy are of paramount concern. With electricity, there is no interest in individual electrons. With information, the key issues are identity, security, and privacy. The side issues are one's inherent identity attributes (such as age, gender, and race), accountability (for online computing activities), and anonymity (in order to preserve free speech and other forms of behavior for the parties involved). The main consideration may turn out to be a matter of control, because from an organizational perspective, control over information has historically been with the organization that creates or maintains it. From a personal perspective, on the other hand, a person should have the wherewithal to control their identity and the release of information about themselves, and in the latter case, a precise determination of to whom it is released and for what reason.. Who owns the data? Is it the person about whom the data pertains? Is it the organization that prototypically manages the data? Or, is it the cloud provider that physically stores the data somewhere out in cyberspace? Consider your financial information. Is it your property or is it your bank's business property? We will try to provide a perspective on this important issue in the following sections. Privacy issues are not fundamentally caused by cloud computing, but they are exacerbated by employing the technology for economic benefit. To put it as diplomatically as possible, if a business employs cloud computing to save money on its IT bill, should it be allowed to do so at the "privacy" expense of its customers?

CLOUD COMPUTING CONCEPTS

Cloud computing is an architectural model for deploying and accessing computer facilities via the Internet. A cloud service provider would supply ubiquitous access through a web browser to software services executed in a cloud data center. The software would satisfy consumer and business needs. Because software availability plays a major role in cloud computing, the subject is often referred to as *software-as-a-service* (SaaS). Conceptually, there is nothing particularly special about a cloud data center, because it is a conventional web site that provides computing and storage facilities. The definitive aspect of a cloud data center is the level of sophistication of hardware and software needed to scale up to service a large number of customers. Cloud computing is a form of service provisioning where the service provider supplies the network access, security, application software, processing capability, and data storage from a data center and operates that center as a utility in order to supply on-demand self-service, broad network access, resource pooling, rapid application acquisition, and measured service. The notion of measured service represents a "pay for what you use" metered model applied to differing forms of customer service.

Cloud Service Characteristics

The operational environment for cloud computing supports three categories of informational resources for achieving agility, availability, collaboration, and elasticity in the deployment and use of cloud services that include software, information, and cloud infrastructure. The *software category* includes system software, application software, infrastructure software, and accessibility software. The *information category* refers to large collections of data and the requisite database and management facilities needed for efficient and secure storage utilization. The *category of cloud infrastructure* is comprised of computer resources, network facilities, and the fabric for scalable consumer operations. We are going to adopt a description of a cloud framework that necessarily includes three forms of description: terminology, architectural requirements, and a reference model. The description generally adheres to the National Institute of Standards and Technology (NIST) cloud-computing paradigm. (Mell 2009b, Brunette 2009)

Agility generally refers to the ability to respond in a timely manner to market and product changes through business alignment, which is achieved by decreasing the lead time to deploy a new application by reducing or eliminating the effect of training, hardware acquisition, and software acquirement. Thus, the IT department is able to respond more quickly to business needs. *Availability* concerns two aspects of computer utilization: the time that the facilities are available for use and the scope of the resources that are available. Cloud computing facilitates *collaboration* through network access, provided that the software tools for end user cooperation are available. *Elasticity* is the characteristic of cloud services that permits computing and storage capability to be scaled up to meet demands on an on-demand basis through resource pooling.

Based on this brief assessment, we can characterize cloud computing as possessing the following characteristics: (Nelson 2009)

- On-demand self service
- Broad network access
- Resource pooling
- Rapid elasticity
- Measured service

The benefit of having lower costs and a less complex operating environment is particularly attractive to small-to-medium-sized enterprises, certain governmental agencies, research organizations, and many countries.

Cloud Computing Utilization

There are four main actors – so to speak – in cloud computing: the cloud service provider, the software service provider, the customer, and the user. Each of the actors represents centers of computer-related activity that can overlap to some degree. The *cloud service provider* (CSP) owns the infrastructure, hardware, software, and network facilities needed to supply cloud computing services managed by a cloud operating system. The CSP performs a function known as *hosting* that can be used to run computer programs, referred to as applications. This facility, known in some circles, as a *cloud platform* (CP), can be regarded as an application service that runs in the cloud. More specifically, a cloud platform provides services to applications in the same manner that "software as a service" programs provide services to clients using the cloud as a transport medium. A cloud platform is as much about operating in the cloud, as it is about developing applications for the cloud. A *software service provider* develops applications that are used by customers to obtain computing services. The SSP can be an independent software vendor (ISV) or an organization that develops a software package that uses the CP as a delivery vehicle for computing and provides application services to customers. ISV software can be used by many customers in the usual fashion for software deployment. When it is shared during operation to achieve economy-of-scale, it is regarded as a multi-tenant model, wherein each customer is one of the tenants. The *customer* (C) is typically an enterprise that is comprised of several employees that use the application and are regarded as users. The *user* (U) is probably going to be a person that uses the cloud computing service via a web browser in one of the following capacities: as an employee of an organization that is contracted to use SaaS provided by an ISV or acquired independently to run in the cloud on a cloud platform; or as a user of third-party SaaS developed by an ISV or the CSP. The four relevant scenarios are summarized by the following schema:

CSP – CP – ISV – C – U
CSP – CP – ISV – U
CSP – CP – C – U
CSP – CP – U

For example, you will be using scenario CSP – CP – ISV – C – U if your company has acquired an operational package from a software vendor and is hosting that software in the cloud. Similarly, you will be using scenario CSP – CP – U if you are using an office package provided by a CSP and accessed via your browser. This form of conceptualization is important from a privacy point-of-view, because each exchange between modules represents a touch point for privacy concerns.

Cloud Platform

A cloud platform provides the facility for an application developer to create applications that run in the cloud or use cloud platform services that are available from the cloud. Chappell lists three kinds of cloud services: SaaS user services, on-premises application development services (attached services), and cloud application development services. (Chappell 2009) An *SaaS application* runs entirely in the cloud and is accessible through the Internet from an on-premises browser. *Attached services* provide functionality through the cloud to support service-oriented architecture (SOA) type component development that runs on-premises. *Cloud application development services* support the development of applications that typically interact while running in the cloud and on-premises.

A cloud platform can be conceptualized as being comprised of three complementary groups of services: foundations, infrastructure services, and application services. The *foundation* refers to the operating system, storage system, file system, and database system. *Infrastructure services* include authorization/authentication/security facilities, integration between infrastructure and application services, and online storage facilities. *Application services* refer to ordinary business services that expose "functional" services as SOA (Service-Oriented Architecture)components. Cloud platforms are a lot like enterprise-level platforms, except that they are designed to scale up to support Internet-level operations.

CLOUD ARCHITECTURE

Cloud architecture is a collection of three categories of information resources for the deployment and use of cloud services that include software, information, and cloud infrastructure. (Katzan 2009) The software category includes system software, application software, infrastructure software, and accessibility software. The information category refers to large collections of data and the requisite database and management facilities needed for efficient and secure storage utilization. The category of cloud infrastructure includes compute resources, network facilities, and the fabric for scalable consumer operations. We are going to adopt an ontological formulation to the description of a cloud framework that necessarily includes three classes of information: terminology, architectural requirements, and a reference model. The description generally adheres to the National Institute of Standards and Technology (NIST) cloud-computing paradigm. (Mel op cit)

Service Models

The cloud service models give a view of what a cloud service is. It is a statement of being. A cloud service system is a set of elements that facilitate the development of cloud applications. (Youseff 2009) Here is a description of the three layers in the NIST service model description: (Mel op cit.)

Cloud Software as a Service (SaaS). The capability provided to the consumer is to use the provider's applications running on a cloud infrastructure. The applications are accessible from various client devices through a thin client interface such as a web browser (e.g., web-based email). The consumer does not manage or control the underlying cloud infrastructure including network, servers, operating systems, storage, or even individual application capabilities, with the possible exception of limited user-specific application configuration settings.

Cloud Platform as a Service (PaaS). The capability provided to the consumer is to deploy onto the cloud infrastructure consumer-created or acquired applications created using programming languages and tools supported by the provider. The consumer does not manage or control the underlying cloud infrastructure including network, servers, operating systems, or storage, but has control over the deployed applications and possibly application hosting environment configurations.

Cloud Infrastructure as a Service (IaaS). The capability provided to the consumer is to provision processing, storage, networks, and other fundamental computing resources where the consumer is able to deploy and run arbitrary software, which can include operating systems and applications. The consumer does not manage or control the underlying cloud infrastructure but has control over operating systems, storage, deployed applications, and possibly limited control of select networking components (e.g., host firewalls).

The three service model elements should be deployed in a cloud environment with the essential characteristics in order to achieve a cloud status.

Service Deployment Models

The essential elements of a cloud service system are given above. In order to develop enterprise-wide applications, a domain ontological viewpoint has to be assumed with deployment models from the following list: (Mel op cit.)

> *Private cloud.* The cloud infrastructure is operated solely for an organization. It may be managed by the organization or a third party and may exist on premise or off premise.

> *Community cloud.* The cloud infrastructure is shared by several organizations and supports a specific community that has shared concerns (e.g., mission, security requirements, policy, and compliance considerations). It may be managed by the organizations or a third party and may exist on-premises or off-premises.

> *Public cloud.* The cloud infrastructure is made available to the general public or a large industry group and is owned by an organization selling cloud services.

> *Hybrid cloud.* The cloud infrastructure is a composition of two or more clouds (private, community, or public) that remain unique entities but are bound together by standardized or proprietary technology that enables data and application portability (e.g., cloud bursting for load-balancing between clouds).

Most cloud software service application domains will be synthesized from a combination of the deployment models.

CLOUD SECURITY

The scope of cloud security is huge by any objective measure. One ordinarily thinks of cloud security in terms of authorization, authentication, accountability, end-to-end trust, and so forth. However, it is important to view cloud security concerns in a broader context of data protection, disaster recovery, and enterprise continuity. The storage of customer data may be useful for operations and research but also opens the door for misuse and violation of privacy policy. Government regulations, such as the FFIEC (Federal financial Institutions Examination Council), HIPAA (Health Insurance Portability and Accountability Act), and PCI DSS (Payment Card Industry Data Security Standards), are in place and strict adherence to the guidelines by cloud service providers can only be achieved through systems design and effective auditing, (Web Hosting Fan 2009) Accordingly, even though we are going to concentrate on the former, it is important to keep the latter in mind through PCI DSS, SOX, and HIPAA compliance. This can be achieved through ISO/IEC 27001:2005 certification and SAS 70 Type I and II attestations. (Shinder 2009) In this section, we are going to develop an operational basis for cloud computing privacy based on security.

Identity

Identity is a means of denoting an entity in a particular namespace and is the basis of security and privacy – regardless if the context is digital identification or non-digital identification. We are going to refer to an identity object as an *entity*. An entity may have several identities and belong to more than one namespace. An identity denotation is based on attributes as suggested by Figure 1.

Figure 1. Conceptual relationship between entities, identities, and attributes.

A pure identity denotation is independent of a specific context, and a federated identity reflects a process that is shared between identity management systems. When one identity management system accepts the certification of another, a phenomenon known as "trust" is established. The execution of trust is often facilitated by a third party that is acknowledged by both parties and serves as the basis of digital identity in cloud services.

Access to computing facilities is achieved through a process known as authentication, whereby an entity makes a claim to its identity by presenting an identity symbol for verification and control. Authentication is usually paired with a related specification known as authorization to obtain the right to address a given service.

Authentication

In a cloud computing environment, an SaaS service provider is commonly faced with two situations: the single tenant model and the multi-tenant model. In the single tenant model, typified by the [CSP – CP – C – U] and [CSP – CP – U] scenarios, given previously, a single sign-on to the cloud service is ordinarily required. This means that the end user would then have to log on to the local computer and then log on to the application service at the cloud platform. This is typically the case with consumer cloud services and customer-developed application software. When the application requires an additional sign-on, it must maintain its own user accounts – a process known as *delegated administration*. This instance is depicted in Figure 2.

When authentication requires a sign-on to an enterprise system running on the cloud and then on to a specific application, a multiple sign-on would ordinarily be required. With a decentralized

HARRY KATZAN JR.

authentication system, as suggested by Figure 3, the user would sign-on to an authentication server that would issue a token accepted by a federated server as proof of identity, required by specific applications. An SaaS provider with thousands of customers would prefer a decentralized solution in lieu of establishing a trust relationship with each of its customers.

Common authenticators are something you know, something you have, something you are, and where you are.

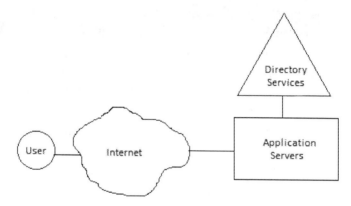

Figure 2. Centralized authentication system.

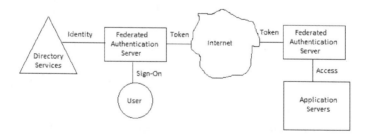

Figure 3. Decentralized authentication system.

Authorization

Typically, *authorization* refers to permission to perform certain actions. In cloud computing, users are assigned roles that must match corresponding roles associated with a requisite SaaS application. Each

SaaS application contains a set of roles pertinent to the corresponding business function. Access is further controlled by business rules that specify conditions that must be met before access is granted. The role/business-rule modality also applies to storage in the cloud, and this is where the practice of privacy kicks in.

In general, the combination of identification and authentication determine who can sign-on to a system – that is, who is authorized to use that system. Authorization, often established with access control lists, determines what functions a user can perform. A related measure, known as accountability, records a user's actions. Authorization cannot occur without authentication.

In general, there are two basic forms of access control: discretionary access control, and mandatory access control. With discretionary access control (DAC), the security policy is determined by the owner of the security object. With mandatory access control (MAC), the security policy is governed by the system that contains the security object. Privacy policy should, in general, be governed by both forms of access control. DAC reflects owner considerations, and MAC governs inter-system controls.

Accountability

Accountability is determined by audit trails and user logs that are prototypically used to uncover security violations and analyze security incidents. In the modern world of computer and information privacy, accountability would additionally incorporate the recording of privacy touch points to assist in managing privacy concerns. Although the Internet is a fruitful technology, it garners very little trust. Why? It is very cumbersome to assign responsibility for shortcomings and failure in an Internet operational environment. Failure now takes on an additional meaning. In addition to operational failure, it is important to also include "failure to perform as expected," as a new dimension.

Trustworthy Computing

Trustworthy computing refers to the notion that people in particular and society as a whole can trust computers to safeguard things that are important to them. Medical and financial information are cases in point. Computing devices, software services, and reliable networks are becoming pervasive in everyday life, but the lingering doubt remains over whether or not we can trust them. Expectations have risen with regard to technology such that those expectations now encompass safety, reliability, and the integrity of organization that supply the technology. Society will only accept a technological advance when an efficient and effective set of policies, engineering processes, business practices, and enforceable regulation are in place. We are searching for a framework to guide the way to efficacy in computing.

It is generally felt that a framework for understanding a technology should reflect the underlying concepts required for its development and subsequent acceptance as an operational modality. A technology should enable the delivery of value rather than constrain it, and that is our objective with trustworthy computing. Security has changed with the advent of the Internet and the well-publicized threats to computing and storage facilities. In the past, security was primarily concerned with keeping harmful people out. In the modern world of the Internet, the objective is to enable the right people to access the right information in a trusted environment. Thus, security is an enabler for greater freedom and confidence in information systems.

As with many utilities, trustworthy computing should be intuitive, controllable, reliable, and predictable. In order to achieve these lofty goals, we are going to look to the framework developed at Microsoft (Mundie 2002) consisting of goals, means, and execution. The set of *goals* reflects a subject's perspective and is comprised of security, privacy, reliability, and business integrity considerations. The set of *means* refers to the computer industry's viewpoint and includes secure-by-design, secure-by-default, secure-in-deployment, fair-information principles, availability, manageability, accuracy, usability, responsiveness, and transparency. *Execution* concerns the manner in which an organization does business and includes intent, implementation, evidence, and integrity. One approach to using the framework is through the concept of a *trusted stack* constructed from five important elements: secure hardware, a trusted operating system, trusted applications, trusted people, and trusted data. (Charney 2008)

A simple view of trustworthy computing is that it is comprised of security, privacy, and usability. Usability and security have been introduced. All that is required to achieve essential trust in cloud computing is privacy.

CLOUD PRIVACY

The cloud will typically process and store information about which privacy is of paramount concern. The main issue is identity, which serves as the basis of privacy or lack of it, and undermines the trust of individuals and organizations in other entities. The key consideration may turn out to be the integrity that organizations adopt when handling personal information and how accountable they are about their information practices. From an organizational perspective, control over information should remain with the end user or the data's creator with adequate controls over repurposing. From a personal perspective, the person should have the wherewithal to control his or her identity as well as the release of socially sensitive identity attributes. Who owns the data? Is it the person about whom the data pertains? Is it the organization that prototypically stores the data? Or, is it the cloud provider that physically stores the data somewhere out in cyberspace? As an example, is your financial information (as personal data) your property or is it your bank's business property?

Key Factors in Privacy Protection

One of the beneficial aspects of the present concern over information privacy is that it places the person about whom data are

HARRY KATZAN JR.

recorded in proper perspective. Whereas such a person may be the object in an information system, he or she is regarded as the subject in privacy protection. This usage of the word *subject* is intended to imply that a person should in fact have some control over the storage of personal information.

More specifically, the *subject* is the person, natural or legal, about whom data are stored. The *beneficial user* is the organization or individual for whom processing is performed, and the *agency* is the computing system in which the processing is performed and information is stored. In many cases, the beneficial user and the subject are members of the same organization. In most instances, however, this will not be the case. For example, the agency may be a service company, and the subject may be a creditor.

In general, the beneficial user obtains value from the data processed and has some control over the manner and time span in which the processing is performed. The agency need not be aware of the end use of the information or how and when the processing is performed.

The heart of the issue is *privacy protection*, which normally refers to the protection of rights of individuals. While the concept may also apply to groups of individuals, the individual aspect of the issue is that which raises questions of privacy and liberty

Privacy Theory

Privacy refers to the claim of persons to determine when, how, and to what extent information about themselves is communicated to others. Much of the literature is concerned with the physical state of being private. The four states of being private are solitude, intimacy, anonymity, and reserve. *Solitude* implies physical separation from the group. *Intimacy* implies participation in a small unit that achieves corporate solitude. *Anonymity* implies freedom from identification and surveillance, which may be informational or physical. *Reserve* implies the creation of a psychological barrier that protects the individual from unwanted intrusion. (Katzan 1980)

The fourth chapter entitled **Compatibility Relations in Identity Analysis** continues with the mathematical treatment of identity by relating constituent namespaces.

The fifth chapter entitled **Conspectus of Cloud Computing** introduces the business value of cloud computing and provides a context for subsequent studies of the subject.

The sixth chapter entitled **Cloud Computing Economics: Democratization and Monetization of Services** gives information on the monetization and democratization of cloud computing services.

The seventh chapter entitled **Ontological View of Cloud Computing** gives a more formal treatment of cloud computing with an emphasis on the language elements of cloud computing.

The eighth chapter entitled **Privacy as a Service** covers why privacy is so important in everyday life and why society should provide "privacy as a service."

The ninth chapter, entitled **Liberty, Freedom, and Rights,** covers why it is necessary to view privacy and identity in a larger context of liberty, freedom, and rights. An individual who is free can select goals, appropriate alternatives, and is not restricted in thought or action by the will or presence of another person. The paper covers the classic struggle between liberty and authority.

The tenth and last chapter, entitled **Global Data Regulation,** covers the ubiquitous use of computers and communications technology, and the transfer of data across worldwide boundaries, in the context of social, economic, and political conditions related to the transborder flow of personal information.

The Appendix gives the United States Privacy Act, and the addendum provides a combined list of references.

It is hoped that this little book will give some exposure to the topics and generate interest in an important facet of modern computing.

HARRY KATZAN, JR.

PREFACE

This book is a collection of short chapters on three important topics: Cloud computing, privacy, and identity. The topics are related but have a separate focus.

Cloud computing is a model for providing on-demand access to computing service via the Internet. The Internet is the connection between a client and a service located somewhere in cyberspace, as compared to having computer applications residing on an "on premises" computer. Cloud computing eliminates two problems in providing computer service: the upfront costs of acquiring computational resources and the time delay of building and deploying software applications. The technology is not without a downside, which, in this case, is the privacy of business and personal information that links the constituent topics together.

The chapters are intended to be read separately resulting in a minor amount of definitional material being repeated. The reader is able to comfortably read the papers on a topic of interest and disregard the remainder.

The first chapter entitled **The Privacy of Cloud Computing** sets the stage for the compendium by establishing the link between cloud computing and privacy. It contains good reference material on the subject matter.

The second chapter paper entitled **Identity as a Service** covers the complex topic of personal identity, which has been an important for philosophers and scientists.

The third chapter entitled **Identity Analytics and Belief Structures** continues with the subject of identity by using mathematical techniques for dealing with identity management and categorizing subjects.

The states serve to provide personal autonomy, emotional release, self evaluation, and limited and protected communication. Privacy is needed to realize basic personal and organizational objectives. Also, there is a universal tendency of individuals to invade the privacy of others and of society as a whole to engage in surveillance to enforce its norms.

Privacy Domain

Personal information is being collected about individuals through information and communication technology inherent in most social and economic activities. When we search the Web, our search phrases are being stored for possible analysis and review. (Conti 2009) When we drive our cars, our license plate numbers and locations are stored by law enforcement. When we purchase items with a credit card, a record of our activity is available to organizations with authority. The list could go on and on, but is well summarized by Ann Cavoukian in Privacy in the Cloouds:

> Our digital footprints are being gathered together bit by bit, megabyte by megabyte, terabyte by terabyte, into personas and profiles and avatars – virtual representations of us, in a hundred thousand simultaneous locations. ... novel risks and threats are emerging from this digital cornucopia. Identity fraud and theft are the diseases of the Information Age, along with new forms of discrimination and social engineering made possible by the surfeit of data.

There are other considerations to the subject of privacy. The majority of companies doing business online and not-online have privacy policies in place that do little to protect consumer privacy. (ACLU 2010, p. 8) The policies give wide latitude to the companies and essentially provide nothing more than informing the consumer of what do, as if telling constitutes legality. The consumer is given few choices to control personal information. In fact, the current situation concerning privacy is that the consumer wants greater control over their information, and a 2009 study found that 69% of adult Internet consumers want the legal right to know everything that a company knows about them. (ACLU op cit.)

Privacy Assessment

The Federal Bureau of Investigation (U.S.A.) lists seven criteria for evaluating privacy concerns for individuals and for designing cloud computing applications: (FBI 2004)

- What information is being collected?
- Why is the information being collected?
- What is the intended use of the information?
- With whom will the information be shared?
- What opportunities will individuals have to decline to provide information or to consent to particular uses of the information?
- How will the information be secure?
- Is this a system of records?

Since privacy is a fundamental right in the United States, the above considerations obviously resulted from extant concerns by individuals and privacy rights groups. In a 2009 Legislative Primer, the following concerns are expressed by the Center for Digital Democracy: (CDD 2009, p. 2)

> **Tracking people's every move online is an invasion of privacy.** Online behavioral tracking is even more distressing when consumers aren't aware who is tracking them, that it's happening, or how the information will be used. Often consumers are not asked for their consent and have no meaningful

control over the collection and use of their information, often by third parties with which they have no relationships.

Online behavioral tracking and targeting can be used to take advantage of vulnerable consumers. Information about a consumer's health, financial condition, age, sexual orientation, and other personal attributes can be inferred from online tracking and used to target the person for payday loans, sub-prime mortgages, bogus health cures and other dubious products and services. Children are an especially vulnerable target audience since they lack the capacity to evaluate ads.

Online behavioral tracking and targeting can be used to unfairly discriminate against consumers. Profiles of individuals, whether accurate or not, can result in "online redlining" in which some people are offered certain consumer products or services at higher costs or with less favorable terms than others, or denied access to goods and services altogether.

Online behavioral profiles may be used for purposes beyond commercial purposes. Internet Service Providers (ISPs), cell phone companies, online advertisers and virtually every business on the web retains critical data on individuals. In the absence of clear privacy laws and security standards these profiles leave individuals vulnerable to warrantless searches, attacks from identity thieves, child predators, domestic abusers and other criminals. Also, despite a lack of accuracy, employers, divorce attorneys, and private investigators may find the information attractive and use the information against the interests of an individual. Individuals have no control over who has access to such information, how it is secured, and under what circumstances it may be obtained.

Based on these issues, the primer includes the following recommendations for legislative consideration: (CDD op cit., p. 4)

> Individuals should be protected even if the information collected about them in behavioral tracking cannot be linked to their names, addresses, or other traditional "personally identifiable information," as long as they can be distinguished as a particular computer user based on their profile.

> Sensitive information should not be collected or used for behavioral tracking or targeting. Sensitive information should be defined by the FTC and should include data about health, finances, ethnicity, race, sexual orientation, personal relationships and political activity.

> No behavioral data should be collected or used from children and adolescents under 18 to the extent that age can be inferred.

> There should be limits to the collection of both personal and behavioral data, and any such data should be obtained by lawful and fair means and, where appropriate, with the knowledge or consent of the individual.

> Personal and behavioral data should be relevant to the purposes for which they are to be used.

The purposes for which both personal and behavioral data are collected should be specified not later than at the time of data collection and the subsequent use limited to the fulfillment of those purposes, and with any change of purpose of the data the individual must be alerted and given an option to refuse collection or use.

Personal and behavioral data should not be disclosed, made available or otherwise used for purposes other than those specified in advance except: a) with the consent of the individual; or b) by the authority of law.

Reasonable security safeguards against loss, unauthorized access, modification, disclosure and other risks should protect both personal and behavioral data.

There should be a general policy of openness about developments, practices, uses and policies with respect to personal and behavioral data. Means should be readily available for establishing the existence and nature of personal data, and the main purposes of their use, as well as the identity and usual residence of the data controller.

An individual should have the right: a) to obtain from a behavioral tracker, or otherwise, confirmation of whether or not the behavioral tracker has data relating to him; b) to have communicated to him data relating to him within a reasonable time; at a charge, if any, that is not excessive; in a reasonable manner; and in a form that is readily intelligible to him; c) to be given reasons if a request made under subparagraphs (a) and (b) is denied, and to be able to challenge such denial; and d) to challenge data relating to him and, if the challenge is successful, to have the data erased, rectified, completed or amended.

Consumers should always be able to obtain their personal or behavioral data held by an entity engaged in tracking or targeting.

Every entity involved in any behavioral tracking or targeting activity should be accountable for complying with the law and its own policies.

Consumers should have the right of private action with liquidated damages; the appropriate protection by federal and state regulations and oversight; and the expectation that online data collection entities will engage in appropriate practices to ensure privacy protection (such as conducting independent audits and the appointment of a Chief Privacy Officer).

If a behavioral targeter receives a subpoena, court order, or legal process that requires the disclosure of information about an identifiable individual, the behavioral targeter must, except where otherwise prohibited by law, make reasonable efforts to a) notify the individual prior to responding to the subpoena, court order, or legal process; and b) provide the individual with as much advance notice as is reasonably practical before responding.

The FTC should establish a Behavioral Tracker Registry.

There should be no preemption of state laws.

Accordingly, it would seem that some form of data governance is in order to protect the privacy rights of subjects .

Privacy Analysis of Cloud Computing

In order to integrate the cloud computing and privacy issues, the *World Privacy Forum* has come up with a set of findings that are summarized in the following list:

- Cloud computing has significant implications for the privacy of personal information as well as for the confidentiality of business and government information.
- A user's privacy and confidentiality risks vary significantly with the terms of service and privacy policy established by the cloud provider.
- For some types of information and some categories of cloud computing users, privacy and confidentiality rights, obligations, and status may change when a user discloses information to a cloud provider.
- Disclosure and remote storage may have adverse consequences for the legal status of or protections for personal or business information.
- The location of information in the cloud may have significant effects on the privacy and confidentiality protection of information and on the privacy obligations of those who process or store the information.
- Information in the cloud may have more than one legal location at the same time, with differing legal consequences.
- Laws could oblige a cloud provider to examine user records for evidence of criminal activity and other matters.
- Legal uncertainties make it difficult to assess the status of information in the cloud as well as the privacy and confidentiality protections available to users.
- Responses to the privacy and confidentiality risks of cloud computing include better policies and practices by cloud providers, changes to laws, and more vigilance by users.

Some of the open items in cloud computing privacy that immediately come to mind are listed as follows:

- A business sharing information with a cloud provider.
- Consequences of third party storage for individuals and business.
- Information disclosure to private parties.
- Location of cloud data and local law.
- Change of a cloud provider.
- Cloud provider disclosure obligations.
- Audits, security, and subpoenas.

Based on this analysis, it would seem that consumer-based cloud services would be good candidates for public and community clouds. For business, education, and government, private and hybrid clouds are prudent options until the legal questions can be resolved.

QUICK SUMMARY

1. Cloud computing is a means of accessing computer facilities via the Internet. (The *cloud* is a metaphor for the Internet.)
2. Cloud service facilities are characterized by four key factors: necessity, reliability, usability, and scalability.
3. Software-as-a-service (SaaS) is software deployed as a hosted service and accessed over the Internet.
4. A cloud platform is based on an operating system that runs in the cloud and provides an infrastructure for software development and deployment.
5. Cloud privacy includes a set of complex and comprehensive issues, and users and providers should proceed with caution when moving to the cloud.

REFERENCES

1   ACLU of Northern California. 2010. *Cloud Computing: Storm Warning for Privacy?* www.dotrights.org, (downloaded 3/11/2010).

2   Brunette, G. and R. Mogull (ed). 2009. *Security Guidance for Critical Areas of Focus in Cloud Computing V2.1.* Cloud Security Alliance, December 2009.

3   Cavoukian, A. 2009. *Privacy in the Clouds.* Toronto: Information and Privacy Commission of Ontario (www.ipc.on.ca).

4   Center for Digital Democracy (CDD). 2009. *Online Behavioral Tracking and Targeting: Legislative Primer September 2009.* www.democraticmedia. org/privacy-legislative-primer. (downloaded 3/11/2010).

5   Chong, F. and G. Carraro. 2006. Architecture Strategies for Catching the Long Tail. *Microsoft Corporation.*

6   Chappell, D. 2009. Introducing the Windows Azure Platform. *Microsoft Corporation.*

7   Charney, S. 2008. Establishing End to End Trust. *Microsoft Corporation.*

8   Conti, G. 2009. *Googling Security.* Upper Saddle River, NJ: Addison-Wesley.

9   Federal Bureau of Investigation. 2004. *Privacy Impact Assessment.* www. fbi.gov/biometrics.htm. (downloaded 2/20/2010).

10 Gellman, R. 2009. *Privacy in the Clouds: Risks to Privacy and Confidentiality form Cloud Computing.* World Privacy Forum (February 23, 2009).

11 Katzan, H. 1980. *Multinational Computer Systems: An Introduction to Transnational Data Flow and Data Regulation.* New York: Van Nostrand Reinhold Co.

12 Katzan, H. 2009. Cloud Computing Economics: Democratization and Monetization of Services. *Journal of Business & Economics Research,* 7(6):1-11.

13 Mell, P. and T. Grance. 2009a. The NIST Definition of Cloud Computing. National Institute of Standards and Technology, Information Technology Laboratory, Version 15, 10-7-09. (http://www.csrc.nist.gov/groups/SNS/cloud-comjputing/index.html)

14 Mell, P., Badger, L., and T. Grance. 2009b. Effectively and Securely Using the Cloud Computing Paradigm. National Institute of Standards and Technology, Information Technology Laboratory, 10-7-09. (http://www. csrc.nist.gov/groups/SNS/cloud-comjputing/index.html)

15 Mundie, C., de Vries, P., Haynes, P., and M. Corwine. 2002. Trustworthy Computing. *Microsoft Corporation.*

16 Nelson, M. 2009. Cloud Computing and Public Policy. *Briefing Paper for the ICCP Technology Foresight Forum.* JT03270509, DATI/ICP(2009)17.

17 Shinder, D. 2009. Microsoft Azure: Security in the Cloud. WindowSecurity. com (downloaded 1/27/2010).

18 Web Hosting Fan. 2009. The Security and Privacy Concerns of Cloud Computing. September 24, 2009. www.webhostingfan.com/page/13 (downloaded 3/2/2010).

19 Youseff, L., Butrico, M., and D. Da Silva. 2009. *Toward a Unified Ontology of Cloud Computing.* (Available from the following: (lyouseff@cs.uscb.edu), (butrico@us.ibm.com), and (dilmasilva@us.ibm.com).

2

IDENTITY AS A SERVICE

INTRODUCTION

Identity is a major issue in the security of modern information systems and the privacy of data stored in those systems. Security and privacy concerns are commonly associated with behavioral tracking, personal-identifiable information (PII), the relevance of private data, data repurposing, and identity theft. We are going to approach the subject from a cloud computing perspective, recognizing that the inherent problems apply to information systems, in general. Cloud computing is a good delivery vehicle for underlying security and privacy concepts, because data is typically stored off-premises and is under the control of a third-party service provider. When a third party gets your data, who knows what is going to happen to it? The main consideration may turn out to be a matter of control, because from an organizational perspective, control over information has historically been with the organization that creates or maintains it. From a personal perspective, on the other hand, a person should have the wherewithal to control their identity and the release of information about themselves, and in the latter case, a precise determination of to whom it is released and for what reason. Privacy issues are not fundamentally caused by technology, but they are exacerbated by employing the technology for economic benefit. After a brief review of cloud computing, security, and privacy to set the stage, we are going to cover identity theory, identity requirements, and an identity taxonomy. This is a working paper on this important subject.

Cloud Computing Concepts for Identity Services

Cloud computing is an architectural model for deploying and accessing computer facilities via the Internet. A cloud service provider would supply ubiquitous access through a web browser to software services executed in a cloud data center. The software would satisfy consumer and business needs. Because software availability plays a major role in cloud computing, the subject is often referred to as *software-as-a-service* (SaaS). Conceptually, there is nothing particularly special about a cloud data center, because it is a conventional web site that provides computing and storage facilities. The definitive aspect of a cloud data center is the level of sophistication of hardware and software needed to scale up to serve a large number of customers. Cloud computing is a form of service provisioning where the service provider supplies the network access, security, application software, processing capability, and data storage from a data center and operates that center as a utility in order to supply on-demand self-service, broad network access, resource pooling, rapid application acquisition, and measured service. The notion of measured service represents a "pay for what you use" metered model applied to differing forms of customer service.

The operational environment for cloud computing supports three categories of informational resources for achieving agility, availability, collaboration, and elasticity in the deployment and use of cloud services that include software, information, and cloud infrastructure. The *software category* includes system software, application software, infrastructure software, and accessibility software. The *information category* refers to large collections of data and the requisite database and management facilities needed for efficient and secure storage utilization. The *category of cloud infrastructure* is comprised of computer resources, network facilities, and the fabric for scalable consumer operations.

Based on this brief description, we can characterize cloud computing as possessing the following characteristics: on-demand self-service, broad network access, resource pooling, rapid elasticity, and measured service. (Nelson 2009) The benefit of having lower costs and a less complex operating environment is particularly attractive to small-to-medium-sized enterprises, certain governmental agencies, research organizations, and many countries. In this paper, cloud computing is used as a delivery vehicle for the presentation of identity services.

Information Security and Identity

The scope of information security is huge by any objective measure. One ordinarily thinks of information security in terms of identity, authentication, authorization, accountability, and end-to-end trust.

Identity is a means of denoting an entity in a particular namespace and is the basis of security and privacy – regardless if the context is digital identification or non-digital identification. We are going to refer to an identity object as a *subject*. A subject may have several identities and belong to more than one namespace. A pure identity denotation is independent of a specific context, and a federated identity reflects a process that is shared between identity management systems. When one identity management system accepts the certification of another, a phenomenon known as "trust" is established. The execution of trust is often facilitated by a third party that is acknowledged by both parties and serves as the basis of digital identity in cloud and other computer services.

Access to informational facilities is achieved through a process known as *authentication*, whereby a subject makes a claim to its identity by presenting an identity symbol for verification and control. Authentication is usually paired with a related specification known as authorization to obtain the right to address a given service.

Typically, *authorization* refers to permission to perform certain actions. Users are assigned roles that must match corresponding roles associated with a requisite computer application. Each application contains a set of roles pertinent to the corresponding business function. Access is further controlled by business rules that specify conditions that must be met before access is granted. The role/business-rule modality also applies to information storage, and this is where the practice of privacy comes into consideration.

In general, the combination of identification and authentication determines who can sign-on to a system – that is, who is authorized to use that system. Authorization, often established with access control lists, determines what functions a user can perform. Authorization cannot occur without authentication. There are two basic forms of access control: discretionary access control, and mandatory access control. With discretionary access control (DAC), the security policy is determined by the owner of the security object. With mandatory access control (MAC), the security policy is governed by the system that contains the security object. Privacy policy should, in general, be governed by both forms of access control. DAC reflects owner considerations, and MAC governs inter-system controls.

Accountability records a user's actions and is determined by audit trails and user logs that are prototypically used to uncover security violations and analyze security incidents. In the modern world of computer and information privacy, accountability would additionally incorporate the recording of privacy touch points to assist in managing privacy concerns over a domain of interest. Although the Internet is a fruitful technology, it garners very little trust, because it is very cumbersome to assign responsibility for shortcomings and failure in an Internet operational environment. Failure now takes on an additional meaning. In addition to operational failure, it is important to also include "inability to perform as expected," as an additional dimension.

Trustworthy computing refers to the notion that people in particular and society as a whole trust computers to safeguard things that are important to them. Medical and financial information are cases in point. Computing devices, software services, and reliable networks are becoming pervasive in everyday life, but the lingering doubt remains over whether or not we can trust them. Expectations have risen with regard to technology such that those expectations now encompass safety, reliability, and the integrity of organizations that supply the technology. Society will only accept a technological advance when an efficient and effective set of policies, engineering processes, business practices, and enforceable regulations are in place. We are searching for a framework to guide the way to efficacy in computing.

It is generally felt that a framework for understanding a technology should reflect the underlying concepts required for its development and subsequent acceptance as an operational modality. A technology should enable the delivery of value rather than constrain it, and that is our objective with identity service

Privacy Concepts

Information systems typically process and store information about which privacy is of paramount concern. The main issue is identity, which serves as the basis of privacy or lack of it, and undermines the trust of individuals and organizations in other information-handling entities. The key consideration may turn out to be the integrity that organizations display when handling personal information and how accountable they are about their information practices. From an organizational perspective, control over information should remain with the end user or the data's creator with adequate controls over repurposing. From a personal perspective, the person should have the wherewithal to control his or her identity as well as the release of socially sensitive identity attributes. One of the beneficial aspects of the present concern over information privacy is that it places the person about whom data are recorded in proper perspective. Whereas such a person may be the object in an information system, he or she is regarded as the subject in privacy protection – as mentioned earlier. This usage of the word *subject* is intended to imply that a person should, in fact, have some control over the storage of personal information.

More specifically, the *subject* is the person, natural or legal, about whom data is stored. The *beneficial user* is the organization or individual for whom processing is performed, and the *agency* is the computing system in which the processing is performed and information is stored. In many cases, the beneficial user and the subject are members of the same organization.

The heart of the issue is *privacy protection*, which normally refers to the protection of rights of individuals. While the concept may also apply to groups of individuals, the individual aspect of the issue is that which raises questions of privacy and liberty

Privacy Assessment

The Federal Bureau of Investigation (U.S.A.) lists several criteria for evaluating privacy concerns for individuals and for designing cloud computing applications: (FBI 2004)

- *What information is being collected?*
- *Why is the information being collected?*
- *What is the intended use of the information?*
- *With whom will the information be shared?*
- *What opportunities will individuals have to decline to provide information or to consent to particular uses of the information?*
- *How will the information be secure?*
- *Is this a system of records?*

Since privacy is a fundamental right in the United States, the above considerations obviously resulted from extant concerns by individuals and privacy rights groups. In a 2009 Legislative Primer, the following concerns are expressed by the Center for Digital Democracy: (CDD 2009, p. 2)

- Tracking people's every move online is an invasion of privacy.
- Online behavioral tracking and targeting can be used to take advantage of vulnerable consumers.
- Online behavioral tracking and targeting can be used to unfairly discriminate against consumers.
- Online behavioral profiles may be used for purposes beyond commercial purposes.

We are going to add to the list that the very fact that personal data is stored online is a matter of concern and should be given serious attention. Based on these issues, this paper is going to take a comprehensive look at the subject of identity in computer and human systems.

IDENTITY THEORY

The notion of identity is an important subject in philosophy, mathematics, and computer information systems. In its most general sense, identity refers to the set of characteristics that makes a subject definable. Each characteristic can be viewed as a single point in a three-dimensional Cartesian coordinate system where the axis are *subject, attribute,* and *value.* (Katzan 1975) Thus, the fact that George is twenty-five years old could be denoted by the triple <George, age, 25>. A set of characteristics over a given domain can uniquely identify a subject. This simple concept is the basis of privacy and identity in cloud computing, information systems, and everyday life. The notion of identity applies to organizational subjects as well as to person subjects.

Knowledge and Power

The phrase "knowledge is power" is a popular means of expressing the value of information. So popular, in fact, that one would think its origin is the modern age of computers and information technology.

That assumption, however, is not correct. The first reference that could be found is credited to the famous Sir Francis Bacon is his book published in 1605 entitled *Advancement of Learning*, quoted as follows: (Bacon 1605)

> But yet the commandment of knowledge is yet higher than the commandment over the will: for it is a commandment over the reason, belief, and understanding of man, which is the highest part of the mind, and giveth law to the will itself. For there is no power on earth which setteth up a throne or chair of estate in the spirits and souls of men, and in their cogitations, imaginations, opinions, and beliefs, but knowledge and learning.

Knowledge, in the sense that it is information concerning a thing or a person, can be used to further one's endeavors or it can be used to control a subject, thus diminishing its freedom and liberty. The protection of personal privacy is a Fourth Amendment right, and identity is the basis of privacy. The following sections give a philosophical view of identity

Knowledge, Attributes, and Identity

Identity is primarily used to establish a relationship between an attribute or set of attributes and a person, object, event, concept, or theory. The relationship can be direct, based on physical evidence, and in other cases, the relationship is indirect and based on a reference to other entities. In a similar vein, the relationship can be certain or uncertain, and in the latter case, based in deduction or inference. The relationship determines an element of knowledge. For example, the knowledge element "you are in your car" is a statement in which "you" and "your car" are things that exist and the "in" is a relationship. Direct knowledge is known by *acquaintance* and is evidenced by a physical connection. Indirect knowledge is determined through a reference to a particular with which the analyst is acquainted. The form is known as knowledge by *description*. (Russell 1912) *Direct knowledge* is determined through sense data, memory, or introspection. *Indirect knowledge* is determined through a reference to another particular, as in "the person who ran for congress in 2004" or through a form of self-awareness where what goes on in subject's mind, for example, is estimated by an analyst's interpretation based on experience or self-evaluation.

Synthetic knowledge reflects certainty based on evidence inherent in the attribute values at hand. *Analytic knowledge* reflects a degree of uncertainty and is determined by deduction, as in "he is the only person with that 'attribute value'," or by inference based on known particulars, such as "all terrorists have beards." Inference, in this case, could be regarded as a form of derivative knowledge. The value of analytic knowledge is that it enables the analyst to exceed his or her limit of private experience. (Kant 1787) The concepts of knowledge, attributes, and identity are summarized in Table 1.

	Synthetic	**Analytic**
By acquaintance	A particular of which we have direct knowledge.	A particular of which we have knowledge based on deduction.
By description	A particular of which we have indirect knowledge by reference to particular with which we are acquainted.	A particular of which we have indirect knowledge through inference (derivative knowledge).

Table 1. Elements of knowledge and identity.

Numerical and Qualitative Identity

Identity refers to the characteristics that make a subject the same or different. We are going to establish two forms of identity: numerical and qualitative. Two subjects are *numerically identical* if they are the same entity, such that there is only one instance. Two subject (or objects in this case) are *qualitatively identical* if they are copies or duplicates. In the popular movie *The Bourne Identity*, for example, the characters *Jason Bourne* and *David Web* are numerically identical, and the number of subjects is one. So it is with *Superman* and *Clark Kent* in another domain. On the other hand, a set of animals with the same biological characteristics – e.g., a species – are regarded as being qualitatively identical. The notion of qualitative identity is remarkably similar to the modern definition of a *category* informally defined as a collection of entities with the same characteristics, having the same values for the same attributes.

Theory of the Indiscernibles

An important aspect of identity theory is that subjects exhibit features of permanence and change, analogous to sameness and difference mentioned previously. We are going to discuss the concept of temporal identity in the next section. The notion of change implies a subject that undergoes a transformation and also a property that remains unchanged. Both Locke and Hume have proclaimed that change reflects the idea of unity and not of identity. Leibnitz proposed the *Theory of Indiscernibles* suggesting that subjects (i.e., objects or entities) that are indiscernible are identical. (Stroll 1967) The subject of indiscernibles has implications for cloud computing, information systems, and change. To what extent a change in a characteristic denotes a change in identity is an open item at this time and implies that there is a probabilistic aspect to identity.

Russell approaches the subject of identity from an alternate viewpoint, analogous to definite and indefinite articles. Russell proposes that a description may be of two sorts: definite and indefinite. A definite description is a name, and an indefinite description is a collection of objects x that have the property ø, such that the proposition øx is true. (Russell 1919) In the phrase *Dan Brown is a famous author*, for example, 'Dan Brown" is a name and the indefinite description is obvious, leading to the probabilistic link between a subject and a characteristic.

Temporal Identity

There is a rich quantity of philosophical literature on the change of identity over time. Are you the same person you were yesterday? Are there persistent attributes that allow for positive identity between time periods? As alluded to previously, entities in everyday life exhibit features of permanence and change. In the domain of personal identity, address attribute is a primary candidate for change. For example, John Smith lives at 123 Main Street. He moves out and another John Smith moves in. This is distinct possibility in a crowded city. Is there a concept in identity theory for this phenomena? Should an identity system take this eventuality into consideration?

As suggested by Figure 1, there is a form of *attribute duality* between a person subject and an object subject. A subject – an object, such as a residence, in this case – is characterized by who lives there. For example, rich people live on Sutton Place in New York. The discussion leads to four related concepts: endurant identity, perdurant identity, endurant attribute, and perdurant attribute. Clearly, the term *endurant* refers to a noun that does not change, where perdurant refers to one that does. Thus, the identity problem is essentially translated to an operant problem of "recognizing identity."

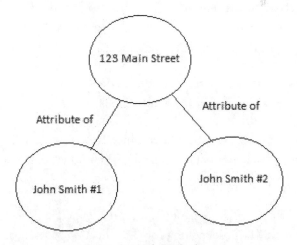

Figure 1 Attribute duality.

IDENTITY REQUIREMENTS

It would appear that there are two essential problems in identity theory: protection of identity and recognition of identity. Protection refers to the safeguarding of one's identity from unwanted intrusion into personal affairs. Recognition refers to the use of identity measures to detect wanted persons. This characterization of the identity problem reflects two sides of the same sword.

Identity Principles

It is generally regarded that effective identity governance should be based on a set of principles to guide the professional activities of IT managers, security officers, privacy officers, and risk management. (Salido 2010, OECD 2010) As delineated, the principles would be based on efficacy in governance, risk management, and compliance with the following objectives:

> **Governance.** Assurance that the organization focuses on basic issues and who is responsible for actions and outcomes.

> **Risk Management.** Assurance that procedures are in place for identifying, analyzing, evaluating, rendering, and monitoring risk.

> **Compliance.** Assurance that actions are within the scope of social and legal provisions.

In accordance with the stated objectives, we can delineate the eight core principles of effective and efficient identity management. (OECD op cit., p.3)

> Principle #1. Collection Limitation Principle – there should be prudent limits on the collection of personal data with the knowledge or consent of the subject.

Principle #2. Data Quality Principle – personal data should be relevant to stated purposes and be accurate, complete, and up-to-date.

Principle #3. Purpose Specification Principle – the purpose of the data collection should be specified beforehand.

Principle #4. Use Limitation Principle – data should be used only for the use specified and not be repurposed.

Principle #5. Security Safeguards Principle – personal data should be safeguarded by reasonable and state-of-the art security facilities.

Principle #6. Openness Principle – the technical infrastructure for protecting personal data should be open as to development, practices, and policies.

Principle #7. Individual Participation Principle – the subject should have the right to definitive information concerning the personal data collected, methods used, and safeguards employed and have the right to challenge the procedures employed.

Principle #8. Accountability Principle – social, business, educational, and governmental data controllers should be required by legal or regularity means to abide by principles 1-8 and be accountable for violations of their provisions.

The eight principles of identity agree in part and parcel to Cavoukian's "7 Laws of Identity, listed as follows without unneeded detail: (Cavoukian 2010) Personal control and consent; Minimal disclosure for limited use; "Need to know access;" User-directed identity; Universal monitoring of the use of identification technology; Human understanding and involvement; and Consistent access and interface to personal data.

Identity and Cloud Computing

Cloud computing hasn't caused the identity problem, but it clearly has exacerbated it, because of limitless flexibility, Internet service provisioning, enhanced collaboration, portability, and easy access. Some of the features that support identity protection are multiple and partial identities, single sign-on, third-part trust relationships, and audit tools that can be used by individuals.

Clearly, there are aspects of cloud computing that need to be addressed.

TAXONOMY OF IDENTITY DATA

Although definitive data does not exist on the subject, there would appear to be an overall distrust on the capability of modern information systems to handle personally-identifiable information (PII). There is also some concern over behavioral tracking, such as purchases and license plate tracking, mistaken identity, erroneous data, and misapplied good intentions – to name only a few instances. So we are going to proceed – at least for this paper – with the assumption that PII data will be collected through various means, both legal and illegal, intentional or unintentional, and by proper means or improper means. We are going to list this data as a basis for further research into the important area of study.

- o Types of identity
  - ▪ Personal information (things that don't change)
    - • Name
    - • SS#
    - • Place of birth

- Date of birth
- Gender
- Race
- Physical characteristics I (Things that don't change)
  - Biometrics
  - Visual image summarization
- Physical characteristics II (Things that don't <u>usually</u> change – at least rapidly)
  - Height
  - Weight
  - Baldness
  - Hair color
- Interpersonal/social identification
  - Marital status
  - Income level
  - Occupation
  - Medical condition
- Psychological characteristics
  - Introvert/extrovert
  - Ectomorph/mesomorph/endomorph
  - Language
- Authentication factors
  - Things you know
  - Something you have
  - Something you are
  - Where you are
  - Something you do
  - Things you do
- General dimensions of PII
  - Temporal
  - Permanent
- Dimensions of identity
  - Personal
  - Social

- Professional
- Behavioral
- Ancestral
- Legal
- Medical
- Governmental
- Educational
- Psychological
- Behavioral identity attributes
  - Where you work
  - Where you travel
  - Where you shop
  - What you purchase
  - What you read
  - What you watch on TV
  - What web sites you access
- Differential attributes
  - What you do for a living
  - Education
  - Where you live
  - Activities
  - Vacation
  - Hobbies
  - Where you shop
- Personal attributes
  - Home
  - Car
  - Discretionary purchases
  - Vacation location
  - Life style
  - Friendships
  - What you wear
  - Demeanor
  - Personal care

- o Identity philosophy
  - Analytic
  - Synthetic
- o Profiling and things to get straight
  - What is a property and an attribute?
  - Inference and logic
    - Logical analysis
    - 1st order logic, 2nd order logic, etc.
  - Profile elements and their relationship
  - Relationship of profiling to identity
  - Is there: Identity-as-a-service?
  - If you make a profile, what is in the profile?
    - Is it correct and up-to-date?
    - Is it inclusive?
    - What are the components?
    - Are attributes defined the same? (consistency)
    - Should there be a standard set of attributes with definitions?
    - Reference
    - Comparison
- o Organization of quantitative and qualitative information that varies over time
  - Qualitative time series
  - Quantitative time series
  - Information stacks
  - Informationqueue

REFERENCES

1 Bacon, Sir Francis. 1605. *Advancement of Learning.* (Republished in the *Great Books of the Western World.* Volume 30, Robert Maynard Hutchins, Editor in Chief, Chicago: Encyclopedia Britannica, Inc., 1952).

2 Black, M. 1952. Identity of Indiscernibles. *Mind* 61:153. (Secondary reference.)

3   ACLU of Northern California. 2010. *Cloud Computing: Storm Warning for Privacy?* www.dotrights.org, (downloaded 3/11/2010).

4   Cavoukian, A. 2009. *Privacy in the Clouds.* Toronto: Information and Privacy Commission of Ontario (www.ipc.on.ca).

5   Cavoukian, A. 2010. 7 Laws of Identity: The Case for Privacy-Embedded Laws of Identity I the Digital Age." Toronto: Information and Privacy Commission of Ontario (www.ipc.on.ca).

6   Center for Digital Democracy (CDD). 2009. *Online Behavioral Tracking and Targeting: Legislative Primer September 2009.* www.democraticmedia.org/privacy-legislative-primer. (downloaded 3/11/2010).

7   Federal Bureau of Investigation. 2004. *Privacy Impact Assessment.* www.fbi.gov/biometrics.htm. (downloaded 2/20/2010).

8   Kant, I. 1787. *Critique of Pure Reason.* (Republished in *Basic Writings of Kant.* Allen W. Wood, Editor, New York: The Modern Library, 2001).

9   Katzan, H. 1975. *Computer Data Management and Data Base Technology,* New York: Van Nostrand Reinhold Co.

10   Katzan, H. 2010. On the Privacy of Cloud Computing. *International Journal of Management and Information Systems,* (accepted for publication).

11   Nelson, M. 2009. Cloud Computing and Public Policy. *Briefing Paper for the ICCP Technology Foresight Forum.* JT03270509, DATI/ICP(2009)17.

12   OECD 2010. OECD Guidelines on the Protection of Privacy and Transborder Flows of Personal Data. www.oecd.org. (downloaded 3/23/2010).

13   Russell, B. 1912. *The Problems of Philosophy.* (Republished by Barnes & Noble, New York, 2004).

14   Russell, B. 1919. *Introduction to Mathematical Philosophy.* (Republished by Barnes & Noble, New York, 2005).

15   Salido, J. and P. Voon. 2010. A Guide to Data Governance for Privacy, Confidentiality, and Compliance: Part 1. The Case for Data Governance. Microsoft Corporation,

16   Stroll, A. 1967. *Identity.* (Entry in *The Encyclopedia of Philosophy,* Volume 4, Paul Edwards, Editor in Chief, New York: Macmillan Publishing Co., 1967).

17   Bacon, Sir Francis. 1605. *Advancement of Learning.* (Republished in the *Great Books of the Western World.* Volume 30, Robert Maynard Hutchins, Editor in Chief, Chicago: Encyclopedia Britannica, Inc., 1952).

18   Black, M. 1952. Identity of Indiscernibles. *Mind* 61:153. (Secondary reference.)

19   ACLU of Northern California. 2010. *Cloud Computing: Storm Warning for Privacy?* www.dotrights.org, (downloaded 3/11/2010).

20   Cavoukian, A. 2009. *Privacy in the Clouds.* Toronto: Information and Privacy Commission of Ontario (www.ipc.on.ca).

21   Cavoukian, A. 2010. 7 Laws of Identity: The Case for Privacy-Embedded Laws of Identity I the Digital Age." Toronto: Information and Privacy Commission of Ontario (www.ipc.on.ca).

22   Center for Digital Democracy (CDD). 2009. *Online Behavioral Tracking and Targeting: Legislative Primer September 2009.* www.democraticmedia. org/privacy-legislative-primer. (downloaded 3/11/2010).

23   Federal Bureau of Investigation. 2004. *Privacy Impact Assessment.* www. fbi.gov/biometrics.htm. (downloaded 2/20/2010).

24   Kant, I. 1787. *Critique of Pure Reason.* (Republished in *Basic Writings of Kant.* Allen W. Wood, Editor, New York: The Modern Library, 2001).

25   Katzan, H. 1975. *Computer Data Management and Data Base Technology,* New York: Van Nostrand Reinhold Co.

26   Katzan, H. 2010. On the Privacy of Cloud Computing. *International Journal of Management and Information Systems,* (accepted for publication).

27   Nelson, M. 2009. Cloud Computing and Public Policy. *Briefing Paper for the ICCP Technology Foresight Forum.* JT03270509, DATI/ICP(2009)17.

28   OECD 2010. OECD Guidelines on the Protection of Privacy and Transborder Flows of Personal Data. www.oecd.org. (downloaded 3/23/2010).

29   Russell, B. 1912. *The Problems of Philosophy.* (Republished by Barnes & Noble, New York, 2004).

30   Russell, B. 1919. *Introduction to Mathematical Philosophy.* (Republished by Barnes & Noble, New York, 2005).

31   Salido, J. and P. Voon. 2010. A Guide to Data Governance for Privacy, Confidentiality, and Compliance: Part 1. The Case for Data Governance. Microsoft Corporation,

32   Stroll, A. 1967. *Identity.* (Entry in *The Encyclopedia of Philosophy,* Volume 4, Paul Edwards, Editor in Chief, New York: Macmillan Publishing Co., 1967).

3

IDENTITY ANALYTICS
AND BELIEF STRUCTURES

INTRODUCTION

Identity is a major issue in the security of modern information systems and the privacy of data stored in those systems. Security and privacy concerns are commonly associated with behavioral tracking, personal-identifiable information (PII), the relevance of private data, data repurposing, identity theft, and homeland security. We are going to approach the subject from a data analytic viewpoint, where the primary challenge is to use identity in an effective way to determine group membership. Instead of focusing on the protection of identity in this paper, we are going to propose methods for using identity to make essential judgmental decisions.

Identity

Identity is a means of denoting an entity in a particular namespace and is the basis of security and privacy – regardless if the context is digital identification or non-digital identification. We are going to refer to an identity object as a *subject*. A subject may have several identities and belong to more than one namespace. A pure identity denotation is independent of a specific context, and a federated identity reflects a process that is shared between identity management systems. When one identity management system accepts the certification of another, a phenomenon known as "trust" is established. The execution of trust is often facilitated by a third party that is acknowledged by both parties and serves as the basis of digital identity in computer-based information systems and personal recognition is social affairs. (Salido 2010) There is another side to personal recognition. We are often afforded the identity of a person based on the judgment of a third party and are obligated to respond to that assessment. It would seem to be prudent in a civilized society to obtain additional information on the subject and combine the various items of information to obtain a composite view before engendering a timely response to the situation.

Privacy

Information systems typically process and store information about which privacy is of paramount concern. The main issue is identity, which serves as the basis of privacy or lack of it, and undermines the trust of individuals and organizations in other information-handling entities. The key consideration may turn out to be the integrity that organizations display when handling personal information and how accountable they are about their information practices. From an organizational perspective, control over information should remain with the end user or the data's creator with adequate controls over repurposing. From a personal perspective, a person should have the wherewithal to control his or her identity as well as the release of socially sensitive identity attributes. (Cavoukian 2009, 2010, ACLU 2010, CDD 2009, OECD 2010, FBI 2004) One of the beneficial aspects of the present concern over information privacy is that it places the person about whom data are recorded in proper perspective. Whereas such a person may be the object in an information system, he or she is regarded as the subject in privacy protection – as mentioned earlier. This usage of the word *subject* is intended to imply that a person should, in fact, have some control over the storage of personal information.

More specifically, the *subject* is the person, natural or legal, about whom data is stored. The *beneficial user* is the organization or individual for whom processing is performed, and the *agency* is the computing system in which the processing is performed and information is stored. In many cases, the beneficial user and the subject are members of the same organization.

The heart of the issue is privacy protection, which normally refers to the protection of rights of individuals. While the concept may also apply to groups of individuals, the individual aspect of the issue is that which raises questions of privacy and liberty. On the other hand, as in the case of terrorism and homeland security, privacy runs contrary to societal needs. We are going to keep those considerations in mind in this paper.

Belief

Belief is often regarded as a mental state in which a person holds a proposition to be true without necessarily being able to prove its truth to other persons. Even though absolute certainty is not required with belief, a person's set of beliefs can play an important role in the causation of behavior. Belief is associated with rational behavior and behavior that is not totally rational. Belief has a lot to do with a believer's mind. If a representation for belief P exists in a person's mind, then it is an *explicit belief.* If a representation for belief Q does not exist in a person's mind but is based on another proposition P, then it is an *implicit* belief. Beliefs that are based on an associative relationship are usually regarded as implicit beliefs.

Some authors class beliefs as being epistemic versus pragmatic and dispositional versus occurent. (Stanford 2010) With an *epistemic belief,* there is evidence for the belief. With *pragmatic belief,* there are practical reasons for the belief. Having been engaged in terrorist training, for example, would probably yield an epistemic belief that the subject has some inclination for terrorism. Pascal's argument to believe in God is an example of a pragmatic belief. It reads as follows:

"The consequences of failing to believe in Him if he exists (eternal fire and damnation) are much worse than the consequences of believing in Him if he does not exist (sin avoidance and contrition)."

Dispositional belief refers to the supposition that the subject is disposed to possess a certain stance on a topic or is inclined to a particular behavior. *Occurent belief* refers to the assumption that the subject is actually performing a sequence of actions. The penultimate example is also an example of dispositional belief. Direct knowledge, or information obtained from a trusted source, that a subject is performing a certain action is associated with occurent belief. In the latter case, verification of identity may be of some concern and be the difference between "belief in" and "knowledge of."

BELIEF STRUCTURES

We are going to assign subjects to an identity set based on values of attributes that characterize that set. An *identity set* is analogous to a namespace except that we are going to view identity from an analytic basis rather than from a privacy and security perspective. Consider the following scenario:

> *We are trying to identify subjects that belong to a certain group G. We know about the group G and its attributes. We have a paid knowledge source K_1 that informs us that subject A is a member of G. However, K_1 is not always correct, and we know that. We have used K_1 enough to know that he provides us with information when he needs money. We have an intuitive belief of how often he is correct. Fortunately, we have another source K_2 that can supply similar information. K_2 is not as hungry for money as K_1, and his opinion frequently runs contrary to K_1's. We would like to use analytics to combine the information from K_1 and K_2 so as to obtain*

a composite picture of the situation. Our resultant belief of A's membership in G is not the end of the story. The belief that we obtain of A's membership in G could then be propagated down the line to other analytic situations. However, we are going to go beyond the notion that even though subject A possesses G's attributes, it doesn't necessarily indicate that A is a member of identity set G.[1]

We are going to use belief structures, compatibility relations, consensus theory, and belief propagation to attack this problem. Consensus theory is a methodology for combining evidence based on Dempster-Shafer theory (Shafer 1976; Katzan 1992, 2006) and the mathematical combination of evidence (Dempster 1967). Consensus theory has commanded a considerable amount of attention in the scientific and business communities, because it allows a knowledge source to assign a numerical measure to a proposition from a problem space and provides a means for the measures accorded to independent knowledge sources to be combined. Consensus theory is attractive because conflicting, as well as confirmatory, evidence from multiple sources may be combined.

Frame of Discernment

A frame of discernment is a means of representing the possibilities under consideration, as in the following example:

```
V = {medicine, law, education}
```

Clearly, the elements in a frame of discernment are, in fact, propositions that can be interpreted as events or states. Thus, if component s_i of system S over domain V were associated with the

---

[1] Consider the following statements. *All spies wear blue trousers. George wears blue trousers. Therefore, George is a spy.* The analysis does not hold unless we have corroborative evidence.

symbol **law,** then that state is equivalent to the proposition, "The true value of V for component s_i is **law**," or in ordinary language, "s_i prefers **law**." Accordingly, the set S of propositions S_i, $S = \{S_1, S_2, \ldots, S_n\}$ represents the collection of states of a system under analysis. Clearly, at an agreed upon point in time, one proposition is true and the others are false.

The basis of identity analytics is a frame of discernment (Θ). Accordingly, a knowledge source may assign a numerical measure to a distinct element of Θ, which is equivalent to assigning a measure of belief to the corresponding proposition. In most cases, the numerical measure will be a belief assignment. A measure of belief may also be assigned to a subset of Θ or to Θ itself. Consider a frame of discernment Θ and its power set denoted by 2^Θ. Given the frame $\Theta = \{a, b, c\}$, its power set is delineated as: $2^\Theta = \{\{a, b, c\}, \{a, b\}, \{a, c\}, \{b, c\}, \{a\}, \{b\}, \{c\}, \{\phi\}\}$. In identity analytics, a knowledge source apportions a unit of belief to an element of 2^Θ. This belief can be regarded as a mass committed to a proposition and represents a judgment as to the strength of the evidence supporting that proposition. When viewed in this manner, evidence focuses on the set corresponding to a proposition; this set is called a *focal set*. The support for a focal set is a function m that maps an element of 2^Θ, denoted by A, onto the interval $[0,1]$. Given a frame of discernment Θ and function $m: 2^\Theta \to [0,1]$, a support function is defined as: $m(\phi) = 0$, where ϕ is the null set, $0 \le m(A) \le 1, A \subset 2^\Theta$, and $\Sigma\, m(A) = 1$.

A simple support function assigns a measure of belief to the focal set A, as: $m(A) > 0$; $m(\Theta) = 1 - m(A)$; and $m(B) = 0$, for all $B \subset 2^\Theta$ and $B \ne A$. The simple support function for a focal set A assigns a portion of the total belief exactly to A and not to its subsets or supersets. The remainder of the belief is assigned to Θ, because certainty function must add up to 1, $m(\Theta) = 1 - m(A)$. It is possible that a body of knowledge or evidence supports more than one proposition, as in the following case. If $\Theta = \{a, b, c, d\}$, $A = \{a, b\}$, and $B = \{a, c, d\}$, then the evidence supports two focal sets, which in the example, are A and B. If $m(A) = 0.5$ and $m(B) = 0.3$, then $m(\Theta) = 0.2$. A support function with more than one focal set is called a *separable support function*. Separable support functions are normally generated when simple support functions are combined. The notion of combining simple support functions is a practical approach to the assessment of evidence. An analyst obtains information from a knowledge source, and it leads to an immediate conclusion – not with certainty, but with a certain level of belief. This is a straightforward means of handling human affairs and is precisely what people do when analyzing situations in everyday life. If additional information comes in, the various pieces of evidence are combined to obtain a composite picture of the situation.

Compatibility Relations

In this particular instance, we are going to establish relations between three sets and the frames of discernment for K_1, K_2, and A, where the K_i are the knowledge sources and A is the subject. The relations will be represented as:

$$K_1 \rightarrow A$$
$$K_2 \rightarrow A$$

and the frames:

$$A = \{m, n\}$$
$$K_1 = \{r, u\}$$
$$K_2 = \{c, i\}$$

The question is whether A is a member of G, denoted by m, or not a member of G, denoted by n. As far as K_1 is concerned, he might be telling us what he thinks we want to hear, so his judgment is classed as reliable, denoted by r, or unreliable, denoted by u. K_2 is simply correct or incorrect, denoted by c or i, respectively.

We can now establish the requisite compatibility relations, based on the fact that K_1 informs us that A is a member of G, and K_2 informs us that A is not a member of G.

1. If K_1 has based his opinion on credible evidence and is operating in a trustworthy manner, then he is in state r that is compatible with state m for A. If K_1 just needs the money or doesn't have good evidence, then he is in state u that is compatible with both states m and n. Thus, we have the compatibility relation:

$$\{(r, m), (u, m), (u, n)\}$$

2. If K_2 is behaving as normal, and there is no reason at this point not to accept that, then he is in state c that is compatible with state n for A. If K_2 is in state i then all bets are off, and this state is compatible with A's states m and n. We then have the second compatibility relation, which is:

$$\{(c, n), (i, m), (i, n)\}$$

Compatibility relations will allow us to assign belief to the assertions of K_1 and K_2 and propagate that belief through the belief network, resulting in a set of focal sets that can be combined using Dempster's rule in order to obtain a composite picture of the situation. Up to this point, we are working in the problem space for the analysis.

Prior Belief

An analyst assigns a measure of credibility to a knowledge source. In our example, let the belief assigned to K_1 be denoted by p and the belief assigned to K_2 be denoted by q, yielding the following prior belief:

Source	Belief
K_1	$\{[(r), p]. [(r, u), 1-p]\}$
K_2	$\{[(c), q]. [(c, i), 1-q]\}$

Since we are in the problem space, our belief in K_1 and K_2 is invariant.

Belief Propagation

Belief propagation transfers the knowledge from the problem space to the solution space using the compatibility relations, resulting in the following focal sets:

Source	Focal Set
K_1	$\{[(m), p]. [(m, n), 1\text{-}p]\}$
K_2	$\{[(n), q]. [(m, n), 1\text{-}q]\}$

The results of belief propagation assign the mass of the information received from K_1 to (m) and the remainder of the belief is assigned to (m, n), which is the frame, denoted by Θ in the above introduction. A similar argument applies to K_2 such that the mass of that belief is assigned to (n) and Θ, respectively.

Combination of Evidence

Using Dempster's rules of combination (Dempster op cit.), the resulting focal sets can be combined yielding the following assessment in the solution space:

$$\left[(m), \frac{p(1-q)}{1-pq}\right], \left[(n), \frac{(1-p)q}{1-pq}\right]. \left[(m, n), \frac{(1-p)(1-q)}{1-pq}\right]$$

using symbolic math from calculations in *Mathematica*™. Applying the expression to several values of p and q yields the following results:

$K_1(p)$	$K_2(q)$	$K_1 \oplus K_2$
.6	.7	$\{[(m), 0.310], [(n), 0.483], [(m, n), 0.207]\}$
.7	.8	$\{[(m), 0.318], [(n), 0.545], [(m, n), 0.136]\}$
.8	.9	$\{[(m), 0.286], [(n), 0.643], [(m, n), 0.071]\}$
.7	.5	$\{[(m), 0.538], [(n), 0.231], [(m, n), 0.231]\}$

This is what we wanted to show. QED.

SUMMARY

We have introduced the theory of identity and applied it to the combination of knowledge for assessment of whether a subject is a member of a certain group. We have introduced belief structures and a relevant methodology for mapping a problem space into a solution space.

APPENDIX: COMBINATION OF EVIDENCE

A method of combining evidence is known as Dempster's rule of combination (Dempster 1967). Evidence would normally be combined when it is obtained from two different observations, each over the same frame of discernment. The combination rule computes a new support function reflecting the consensus of the combined evidence.

If m_1 and m_2 denote two support functions, then their combination is denoted by $m_1 \oplus m_2$ and is called their *orthogonal sum*. The combination $m_1 \oplus m_2$ is computed from m_1 and m_2 by considering all products of the form $m_1(X) \bullet m_2(Y)$, where X and Y range over the elements of Θ; $m_1(X) \bullet m_2(Y)$ is the set intersection of X and Y combined with the product of the corresponding probabilities.

For example, consider the frame of discernment

$$\Theta = \{h, t, s\}$$

and views A and B, based on two different observations over the same frame:

$$X = \{\{h\},0.6\},\{\{t\},0.3\},\{\{s\},0.1\}\}$$
$$Y = \{\{h\},0.4\},\{\{t\},0.4\},\{\{s\},0.2\}\}$$

The entries are combined, as follows, using Dempster's rule of combination:

$$m_1 \oplus m_2(\{h\}) = 0.24$$
$$m_1 \oplus m_2(\{t\}) = 0.12$$
$$m_1 \oplus m_2(\{s\}) = 0.02$$
$$m_1 \oplus m_2(\{\emptyset\}) = 0.62$$

Thus, for $A_i \cap B_j = A$ and $m_1 \oplus m_2 = m$, the combination rule is defined mathematically as:

$$m(A) = \underset{A_i \cap B_j = A}{\Sigma m_1(A_i) \cdot m_2(B_j)} / (1 - \underset{A_i \cap B_j = \emptyset}{\Sigma m_1(A_i) \cdot m_2(B_j)})$$

The denominator reflects a normalization process to insure that the pooled values sum to 1. So, in this instance, the normalization process yields the combination

$$X \oplus Y = \{\{h\}, 0.63\}, \{\{t\}, 0.32\}, \{\{s\}, 0.05\}\}$$

after normalization by dividing the combined assessment by (1-0.62) or 0.38. Because the problem is well-structured, the representation can be simplified as

$$X \oplus Y = \{0.63, 0.32, 0.05\}$$

For views $A = \{A_1, A_2, ..., A_n\}$ and $B = \{B_1, B_2, ..., B_n\}$, the combination rule can be simplified as

$$A \oplus B = \{A_1{}'B_1/k, A_2{}'B_2/k, ..., A_n{}'B_n/k\}$$

where

$$k = \sum_{i=1}^{n} A_i{}'B_i$$

We will refer to latter the equation as the *simplification rule.* (Katzan 2009) Readers are directed to Shafer (1976) and Katzan (1992) for additional information on Dempster's rule of combination.

REFERENCES

1   Dempster, A.P. 1967, "Upper and Lower Probabilities Induced by a Multivalued Mapping," *The Annals of Statistics* 28:325-339.

2   Federal Bureau of Investigation. 2004. *Privacy Impact Assessment.* www.fbi.gov/biometrics.htm. (downloaded 2/20/2010).

3   Katzan, H. 1992. *Managing Uncertainty: A Pragmatic Approach,* New York: Van Nostrand Reinhold Co.

4   Katzan, H. 2008. Categorical Analytics Based on Consensus Theory. *Journal of Business and Economics Research,* 6(8), 89-102.

5   Katzan, H. 2010. On the Privacy of Cloud Computing. *International Journal of Management and Information Systems,* (accepted for publication).

6   Shafer, G. 1976, *A Mathematical Theory of Evidence,* Princeton, NJ: Princeton University Press.

4

COMPATIBILITY RELATIONS IN IDENTITY ANALYSIS

INTRODUCTION

Identity refers to the categorization of an individual and the assigning of a name to that determination. We are going to approach the subject of identity from a data analytic viewpoint, where the primary challenge is to use identity in an effective way to determine group membership. Methods have been developed for propagating belief through a complex network of belief assessments. The focus of this paper is on compatibility relations, defined as the mapping of belief between identity namespaces. This paper is intended to accompany a related paper entitled "Identity Analytics and Belief Structures." The introductory section contains common material, so it can be read independently.

Identity Concepts

Identity is a means of denoting an entity in a particular namespace and is the basis of analytic behavior analysis. We are often afforded the identity of a person based on the judgment of a third party and are obligated to respond to that assessment. It would seem to be prudent in a civilized society to obtain additional information on the subject and combine the various items of information to obtain a composite view before engendering a timely response to the situation.

Identity is primarily used to establish a relationship between an attribute or set of attributes and a person, object, event, concept, or theory. The relationship can be direct, based on physical evidence, and in other cases, the relationship is indirect and based on a reference to other entities. Direct knowledge is known by *acquaintance* and is evidenced by a physical connection. Indirect knowledge is determined through a reference to a particular with which the analyst is acquainted. This form is known as knowledge by *description*. (Russell 1912) *Direct knowledge* is determined through sense data, memory, or introspection. *Indirect knowledge* is determined through a reference to another particular, as in "the person who was mayor in 2009."

Belief Concepts

Belief is often regarded as a mental state in which a person holds a proposition to be true without necessarily being able to prove its truth to other persons. Even though absolute certainty is not required with belief, a person's set of beliefs can play an important role in the causation of behavior. If a representation for belief P exists in a person's mind, then it is an *explicit belief*. If a representation for belief Q does not exist in a person's mind but is based on another proposition P, then it is an *implicit* belief. Beliefs that are based on an associative relationship are usually regarded as implicit beliefs.

Dispositional belief refers to the supposition that the subject is disposed to possess a certain stance on a topic or is inclined to a particular behavior. *Occurent belief* refers to the assumption that the subject is actually performing a sequence of actions. The penultimate example is also an example of dispositional belief. Direct knowledge, or information obtained from a trusted source, that a subject is performing a certain action is associated with occurent belief. In the latter case, verification of identity may be of some concern and be the difference between "belief in" and "knowledge of."

UNCERTAINTY

Identity and uncertainty are related within the domain of identity analytics and belief propagation. When an analyst believes something but cannot prove it analytically or statistically, he or she is assigning a measure to the strength of the evidence supporting a specific proposition. In the present context, we are interested in the certainty of group membership.

Analytic Behavior

Analytic behavior is based on two related but often conflicting theories of action. At the individual level, people think in a cause-oriented fashion and use information to match existing patterns in order to make sense out of a minimal amount of information. (Campbell 1989, Tversky 1974) The mind too easily forms prototypes and constructs scenarios. At the organizational level, operational knowledge, based on a partial mapping of reality, is developed to determine how an organization responds to external stimuli and generates strategies and actions. Thus, both individuals and organizations do not typically handle uncertainty but respond to it according to existing ideologies. Implicit in this discussion is the not-so-obvious fact that we often have too much information and have a tendency to relate it to existing scenarios regardless of their applicability. In order to execute assessment in a judicious manner, a cognitive process, comprised of selection, processing, and response, is proposed as a context for identity analysis based on uncertainty.

Two forms of information are required to handle uncertainty: indicators from the real world and belief in what those indicators mean. Collectively, the combination of indicators, belief, and meaning is known as *evidence*. Evidence from independent knowledge sources should be combined to construct effective courses of action, as denoted by the lifecycle for belief revision and organizational action. (Katzan 1992)

Based on the degree to which a phenomenological system is accessible to empirical investigation, three modalities have been established: (Sutherland 1975)

- *Empirico-inductive modality* in which facts can be determined from observation and principles can be derived from facts.
- *Hypothetico-deductive modality* in which hypotheses are based on intuition, imagination, and other intellectual methods and deductive methods are used to verify predictions with observations.
- *Knowledge-based modality* that is characterized by key indicators serving as access keys to information structures and response scenarios, as in medical diagnosis, wherein knowledge structures are organized as a complex network of relationships.

Although identity analysis would essentially employ the three modalities, as required, the emphasis would necessarily focus on the knowledge-based modality, since indicators can certainly give some insight into the true state of reality – but not always with certainty.

Uncertain Reasoning

Most information systems treat information as though it was a proven fact, but in actuality, this is rarely the case. In addition, inferences based on so-called exact information are equally uncertain. Valid inference relations should take the form:

if x then y with confidence m

where the confidence factor m reflects the degree of confidence that a domain expert assigned to the inference relation. The uncertainty in this case is the reflection of one or more of the following conditions: (1) Inherent uncertainty in the possibility set; (2) Incomplete evidence; and (3) Incorrect evidence because of measurement errors. The uncertainty, incompleteness, and incorrectness of information are the reasons we wish to model identity information from the viewpoint of uncertain reasoning.

Degrees of Belief

In order to investigate degrees of belief, we are going to employ the following construct:

if x **then** y (to degree a)

and refer to the expression as an inference rule. Here are some examples:

if the patient has a large lump
then there is evidence (0.7) that medical tests are necessary.

if housing starts are up
then there is evidence (0.6) that interest rates will also rise within 6 months.

The certainty factor in an inference rule is an expression of its inherent uncertainty. There is frequently some uncertainty in the antecedents, as well, because of reasons given in the previous section. This prospect is demonstrated in the following example:

if the patient has a large lump (0.7)
and the patient's blood is weak (0.4)
then there is strong evidence (0.9) that the patient should go to the hospital for treatment.

In this example, the evidence of a large lump is uncertain (0.7) because of the vagueness of the word "large," and similarly with the evidence for "weak" blood (0.4). The certainty associated with the rule is, in this case, equal to (0.9).

In the antecedent part of a rule, evidence is combined in accordance with the following definitions for the logical operators:

p **and** q = **min**(p, q) *The smaller*
p **or** q = **max**(p, q) *The larger*
not p = $1-p$ *The inverse*

The rules are then evaluated according to the following steps:

1. If the antecedent is a logical expression, then it is evaluated as covered.
2. The belief for the conclusion produced by a rule is the belief for the antecedent multiplied by the certainty associated with the rule.
3. The belief for a fact produced as the conclusion of one or more rule evaluations is the maximum of the beliefs produced by all of the rules that yield that conclusion.

Example:

Rule 1
if a **and** b **and** c **then** d (certainty = 0.7)

Rule 2
if h **or** i **then** d (certainty = 0.8)

Assume that facts $a, b, c, h,$ and i have beliefs of 0.7, 0.3, 0.5, 0.7, and 0.9, respectively. The following computation produced a belief of 0.72 for d:

min(a, b, c) = min$(0.7, 0.3, 0.5)$ = 0.3   *By step 1*
Belief for rule 1 = $0.3 \times 0.7 = 0.21$ *By step 2*
max(h, i) = max$(0.7, 0.9)$ = 0.9   *By step 1*
Belief for rule 2 = $0.9 \times 0.8 = 0.72$ *By step 2*
max$(Belief\ for\ rule\ 1, Belief\ for\ rule\ 2)$ = 0.72   *By step 3*

This is the inference method used for possibility theory (Fuzzy Set Theory). (Zadeh 1986) The results are not confirmatory but illustrate the gist of belief propagation.

Assignment of Belief

The assignment of belief involves the association of a basic probability assignment to the uncertainty inherent in a mutually exclusive and exhaustive set of possibilities. In some instances, the assignment of belief can be made by using the probability values in another probability space. (Neapolitan 1990)

Consider the task of determining the price of equity DS. Let R stand for the proposition, "The value of DS will rise," and let S represent the proposition, "Sam predicts the value of DS will rise." It would be desirable to have the conditional probability of R given S, i.e., $P(R|S)$, but that information is unfortunately not available through repeated trials.

On the other hand, Sam is a crackerjack analyst, and given that he has performed a thorough fundamental analysis of an equity, it will unquestionably rise if Sam says it will. However, Sam is a busy guy, and coupled with the fact that Sam has quite an ego, the situation sometimes results in Sam giving an investment opinion off the cuff, when he hasn't done his homework. Assume that Sam does his homework 70% of the time and let H represent the proposition, "Sam has done his homework." Thus, $P(H) = 0.70$ in this instance.

We are seeking the probability of R and can use the probabilities in another probability space to infer it. Now if H is true, then events H and R are compatible and we have the relationship:

$$m_1(\{R\}) = P(H) = 0.7$$

where m_1 represents the mass afforded to the enclosed proposition. (Katzan 1992, 2008, 2010) The other 30% of the time, Sam takes an educated guess, so all bets are off. Thus, the complement of H, namely H^c, is compatible with R and R^c, so we have:

$m_1(\{R, R^c\}) = P(H^c) = 0.3$

In this instance, Sam has predicted that DS will rise, i.e., proposition S, and Sam has done his homework. Thus, H and R^c are not compatible. We have used Sam's probability space of H to determine DS's probability space for R.

We can use a similar argument to obtain a second estimate over the frame of discernment $\{R, R^c\}$. Suppose that R is true when the value of the Dow rises, representing the latter proposition by D. Assume the Dow goes up 80% of the time; when it does not, it's another random walk down Wall Street. Thus, we have the relationships:

$m_2(\{R\}) = P(D) = 0.8$
$m_2(\{R, R^c\}) = P(D^c) = 0.2$

As before, D is compatible with R but not with R^c; D^c is compatible with both R and R^c. Using Dempster's rule of combination, we obtain a composite picture of the situation and demonstrate the compatibility relation:

$m = m_1 \oplus m_2$
$m(\{R\}) = 0.94$
$m(\{R, R^c\}) = 0.06$

Information on Dempster-Shafer Theory is given in the accompanying paper (Katzan 2010) and in the relevant publications. (Shafer 1976, Dempster 1967, and Katzan 1992)

COMPATIBILITY RELATIONS

This section gives an algorithm for exercising a compatibility relation between focal sets in two information spaces. A belief system can be conveniently conceptualized as a directed graph (G), represented symbolically as G={V,E}, where V is a set of vertices and

E is a set of edges. The vertices are called *nodes* and the edges are referred to as *links*. The nodes store information that take the form of belief structures. The links represent the relationship between nodes. A *belief system* is a collection of four entities: evidence, nodes, links, and decision scripts.

Evidence

An element of evidence is represented as a simple support function over a frame of discernment and regarded as a "cloud of evidence" that takes the form:

$$e = \{obj_1, obj_2, ..., obj_n), bpa\}$$

where obj_i is an object from the frame of discernment and bpa is a basic probability assignment taken as a measure of belief that a random variable is contained in the belief set. If Θ is the frame of discernment, then $m(A)$ is a measure of belief assigned to a subset A of Θ.

Nodes

A *node* is an abstract structure that serves to hold evidence. In general, there are two types of nodes: those that are linked to the environment and those that are not. Three classes exist:

- *Affector nodes* that obtain their information from clouds of evidence. If the input to an affector node is a single cloud, then that affector node holds a simple support unit. If there are two or more inputs to an affector node, then that evidence is combined using Dempster's rule of combination, and the node holds a separable support unit. An affector node represents an *explicit belief.*
- *Constructor nodes* that exist as internal nodes and have belief propagated to them and also have belief propagated from them. If belief is propagated to a constructor node from two

HARRY KATZAN JR.

or more nodes, then it is always combined using Dempster's rule. A constructor node represents an implicit belief.

- *Effector* nodes that are objects to which external entities are attached, such as with a decision script. An effector node is a means of taking appropriate action if specified conditions are met.

A node may be assigned an initial state and takes the meaning of an explicit belief.

Links

A *link* represents a direction along which belief can be propagated. Consider two frames of discernment Θ^A and Θ^B. Further, assume two corresponding sets of propositions $\{P_j^A\}$ and $\{P_j^B\}$, where $j=1,2,...,m$ and $k=1,2,...,n$. The relation

$$\Theta_j^A \rightarrow \Theta_k^B$$

denotes a linking of frames Θ^A and Θ^B through a set of rules of the form, **if** p_j **then** p_k for couplets p_j^A and p_k^B from frames Θ^A and Θ^B, respectively.

The set of couplets and a probability assignment of the form

$$r_B^A = (((p_1^A, p_1^B)\,(p_2^A, p_2^B)\,(p_3^A, p_3^B)\,...)\,prob_B^A)$$

is known as a "compatibility relation." Θ^A and Θ^B are not necessarily distinct.

Decision Scripts

A decision script translates a resultant belief structure into a prescription for action. We are going to define an *inference relation* of the form

(antecedent, threshold) → (consequent, certainty-value)

It should be interpreted as follows: if the *bpa* of the antecedent exceeds the threshold, replace the antecedent with the consequent and compute its *bpa* (i..e., the new *bpa*) as the product of the antecedent's bpa and the consequent's certainty-value. For example, consider the inference relation

$$(\{a, b\}, 0.6) \rightarrow (\{c, d\}, 0.7)$$

Thus, antecedent of $\{\{a, b\}, 0.8\}$ would map to a consequent of $\{\{c, d\}, 0.56\}$.

Technical Description

In a compatibility relation, a set of rules of the form

if p_j^A then p_k^B

along with a basic probability assignment is represented as

$$r_B^A = (((p_1^A, p_1^B)\ (p_2^A, p_2^B)\ (p_3^A, p_3^B)\ \ldots)\ prob_B^A)$$

Each couplet of the form (p_j^A, p_k^B) denotes that an element p_j^A in Θ^A is replaced by the element p_k^B in Θ^B, denoting the aforementioned mapping from Θ^A to Θ^B.

For example, consider two frames of discernment F_1 and F_2 delineated as follows:

$$F_1 = \{a, b, c\}$$
$$F_2 = \{x, y, z, w\}$$

A focal set defined on F_1 is

$$F_1 = ((a, b), 0.6)$$

Consider the set of rules

> **if** a **then** x
> **if** a **then** y
> **if** b **then** w
> **if** c **then** y
> **if** c **then** z

with a measure of belief of 0.8. This is equivalent to stating the belief that one or more of the rules in the set would hold with a subjective probability of 0.8. The set of rules is expressed as a compatibility relation of the form:

$$r = ((a, x), (a, y), (b, w), (c, y), (c, z)), 0.8)$$

The simple compatibility relation r is applied to the focal set F_1 by replacing each element of F_1, that is elements a and b, by the set of consequents of all rules in which that element is equal to its antecedent. The process is summarized as follows:

1. For each focal element of F_1, i.e., a or b, replace it with the second element of all couplets where the first element matches. Thus, a is replaced with x and y, and b is replaced with w, yielding the focal set (x, y, w) over F_2.
2. Take the product of the probabilities, i.e., 0.6×0.8, as with Dempster's rule.

The sequence of operations yields the support unit

$$((x, y, w), 0.48)$$

which is the projection of F_1 onto F_2. QED.

QUICK SUMMARY

1. This paper is intended to supplement the companion paper entitled *Group Association Using Identity Analysis* in the area of compatibility relations, which is the mapping between two frames of discernment.
2. Introductory material on identity and belief is covered.
3. A technical description of uncertainty theory is given.
4. Compatibility relations as they apply to identity analysis are described.
5. Subordinate topics are covered including evidence, nodes, links, and decision scripts is covered.
6. Numerous examples are given.

REFERENCES

1   Campbell, J. 1989. *The Improbable Machine,* New York: Simon & Schuster, Inc.
2   Dempster, A.P. 1967, Upper and Lower Probabilities Induced by a Multivalued Mapping. *The Annals of Statistics* 28:325-339.
3   Katzan, H. 1992. *Managing Uncertainty: A Pragmatic Approach,* New York: Van Nostrand Reinhold Co.
4   Katzan, H. 2008. Categorical Analytics Based on Consensus Theory. *Journal of Business and Economics Research,* 6(8), 89-102.
5   Katzan, H. 2010. Group Association Using Identity Analysis. *Proceedings of the SE INFORMS Conference.* Myrtle Beach, SC, October 7-8, 2010.
6   Neapolitan, R. 1990. *Probabilistic Reasoning in Expert Systems: Theory and Applications,* New York: John Wiley & Sons, Inc.
7   Shafer, G. 1976, *A Mathematical Theory of Evidence,* Princeton, NJ: Princeton University Press.

5

CONSPECTUS OF CLOUD COMPUTING

INTRODUCTION

As modern business, government, and education have evolved into the 21st century, the use of computers to sustain everyday operations has increased. Most organizations employ computers to enhance core services and provide supplementary services to gain efficacy and efficiency for auxiliary operations. One of the newest technologies for IT provisioning is cloud computing that has garnered a considerable amount of attention in the business, education, and government communities. Many persons in small business and universities are not totally aware of the benefits of cloud computing, and that is the reason for this paper. First, we will cover what cloud computing is; then we will cover how it works; next we will cover how to get it; and finally, we will take a good shot at giving the pros and cons of adopting it as your mode of operation.

Cloud computing is a means of providing computer facilities via the Internet, but that is only half of the picture. The other half is that it is also a means of accessing those same computer facilities via the Internet from different locations. When a large bank, for example, moves to cloud computing for online operations, it necessarily considers both halves of the equation. The adjective "cloud" reflects the diagrammatic use of a cloud as a metaphor for the Internet. In telecommunications, a *cloud* is the unpredictable part of a network through which business and personal information passes from end-to-end and over which we do not have direct knowledge or control.[2]

The value proposition that underlies cloud computing is that an organization does not have to pay the up-front costs of hardware, software, networks, people, training, and other infrastructural elements. Instead, the organization would utilize resources provided on the Internet as they would a service utility, such as electric service and pay only for what it uses. The service would take care of peak periods, support, downtime, training, and a myriad of other things with which an organization would possibly prefer not to get involved. Another important consideration is that many organizations that depend on online services have to plan for a worst-case scenario and experience low server utilization even during peak periods. Some major banks have a server use percentage as low as 6% during normal periods and 20% during peak periods.

The essence of cloud computing is service. The company providing cloud computing service assumes the role of service provider, and the organization using the service takes on the role of the client (or customer) with all of the rights and privileges pertaining thereto. Services are indigenous to the existence of modern society and are constantly being invented and retired. So we should be right at home with cloud computing. At least, that is what major computer and software companies, major financial organizations, the U.S. Government, and the National Institute of Standards and Technology (NIST) seem to think.[3]

CHARACTERISTICS OF CLOUD COMPUTING

Computing is a social phenomena based on technology, the basis of which is input, processing, output, and storage. If the task is an ordinary computer application, such as word processing, payroll, use

---

[2] See *Privacy in the Clouds* by Cavoukin for more information on this subject.
[3] See the NIST definition of cloud computing by Mell and Grance.

of the cell phone, or checkout at the supermarket, there is always the aforementioned four steps known as the *information processing cycle.* In a very general sense, input can come from people and machines, processing is done by computers, output goes to people or machines, and information produced or absorbed during computation can be stored for future use on electronic devices. Where in an organizational sense each of the steps actually takes place determines if it is cloud computing or traditional "on premises" computing. Relying on evolutionary processes, we can observe that the structure of an organism essentially determines its potential for growth. So it is with cloud computing.

A cloud computing service would necessarily have ubiquitous access through a Web browser or mobile device providing the input step. The computing and storage facilities would reside in and operate from a data center in the cloud. The output is returned to the end user through the browser program or mobile device, mentioned previously. In order to sustain the cloud operational environment, a cloud computing service would provide a utility-level infrastructure with the following operational characteristics: necessity, reliability, usability, and scalability. *Necessity* refers to the idea that a preponderance of users depend on the service to satisfy everyday needs. *Reliability* refers to the expectation that the service will be available when the user requires it. *Usability* refers to the requirement that the service is easy and convenient to use – regardless of the complexity of the underlying infrastructure. *Scalability* refers to the fact that the service has sufficient capacity to allow the users to experience the benefits of an expandable service that provides economy of scale. Certainly, modern Internet facilities for search operations that typically engage thousands of servers satisfy these characteristics.

APPLICATION SERVICE PROVISIONING

The need for effective computer service provisioning has been on the sidelines for some time and represents a unrealized requirement in the business, education, and government worlds. The situation is that small to medium-sized organizations have need for expensive computing facilities and software service. A prototypical example is the small software firm that needs occasional mainframe computer time. The solution has been to lease service from an application service provider (ASP) and use that service via network facilities. The ASP supplies the computer time and provides operational software as required. The process is known as *hosting*. The customer assumes the network expenses without the up-front hardware, software, and facilities costs.

With cloud computing, the Internet provides the network facilities. A cloud service provider supplies the computer and operating system resources that can be accessed via the Internet. Applications software is supplied by an independent software vendor (ISV) and therein resides the benefit to the customer. The customer, which can have several users, shares the software among several customers so as to achieve significant economy-of-scale.

BUSINESS AND CONSUMER SERVICE

Chong and Carraro at Microsoft[4] define shared software as *software-as-a-service* (SaaS) deployed as a hosted service and accessed over the Internet. The key features of SaaS are where the programs reside and how they are accessed. The two kinds of software in this category are business software and consumer software. Business software provides business services and emphasizes business solutions, such as customer relationship management (CRM), supply chain management (SCM), enterprise resource planning (ERP), and human resources. Consumer software provides personal solutions, such as office applications, that are often available at no cost in their cloud versions.

With business services, the most important consideration is whether the process is executed in-house or as a cloud service. When the

---

[4] See Chong, 2006.

process is handled in-house, total control over the operation is obtained along with limited opportunity for achieving economy-of-scale. As processes are distributed outward on the cloud, control is decreased but opportunities for achieving economy-of-scale are increased. The considerations are different with consumer services. Pure service, as with office applications, provides practically no control over the application to the client and a reasonably high-level of economy-of-scale to the provider. In many cases, consumer services are advertising-supported and are complimentary to the client through advertising. In addition to metered and subscription models, the advertising-supported model is another means of monetizing cloud computing.

Business applications that reside "on premises" are governed by the traditional considerations of application acquisition and deployment. If an application resides on and is deployed from the cloud, then two options exist:

1. Build the software yourself (or have it built for you) and run it on the cloud as a hosted service – perhaps using a cloud platform.
2. Obtain the application software from an independent software vendor (ISV) and run it on the cloud in a standard or modified mode.

In the former case, all users access the same version of the software. In the latter case, a client gets a customized version achieved with a separate code base (or its equivalent) and configuration options. A note on terminology is in order, especially with regard to line-of-business software. In a prototypical cloud environment, there are multiple service entities providing service, such as the cloud infrastructure provider (i.e., the computer part) and the ISV (i.e., the software part).

The two entities are combined for discussion purposes into a single service provider that we are going to conceptually refer to as the cloud software service (CSS). Two companies, for example, contract with the

CSS for access to and the execution of business applications in areas such as general ledger, treasury management, real estate, and so forth. The companies are referred to as customers of the CSS. Each customer entrusts several employees to use the contracted services, and they are regarded as the users. In some instances, the customers and their respective users are considered to be clients of the service provider.

The primary advantage of a cloud consumer service is that it is typically free to the client, as well as being accessible from any location via the Internet, and it yields advertising-supported revenue for the provider. Consumer services have a near-zero marginal cost of distribution to clients, requiring only a fraction of the number of clients to respond to advertising. This is the well-known *Freemium Business Model*[5], characterized as follows: In the free sample product model, you give away 1% of your product to sell the additional 99%, whereas in the freemium model, you give away 99% to sell 1%.[6] Because of the scale of the Internet with millions of users, you can reach a large market, so that the 1% is a huge amount.

Clearly, the business model for the deployment of SaaS changes with the adoption of cloud computing. The ownership of software shifts from the client to the provider, along with the responsibility for the technology infrastructure and its management[7].

CLOUD PLATFORMS AND SERVICE DEPLOYMENT MODELS

A *cloud platform* is an operating system that runs in the cloud and supports the software-as-a service concept. A cloud platform resides in a cloud data center and exists as a powerful computing facility, a storage system, an advanced operating system, support

---

[5] See Anderson 2006.

[6] The percentages should not be taken literally, in this instance. They are used only to make a point (Anderson 2006).

[7] See Chong 2006.

software, and the necessary fabric to sustain a server farm and scale up to support millions of Internet clients. A cloud platform is as much about operating in the cloud, as it is about developing applications for the cloud. A cloud platform provides the facility for an application developer to create applications that run in the cloud; and, in so doing, the application developer uses services that are available from the cloud. Cloud platforms are a lot like enterprise-level platforms, except that they are designed to scale up to Internet-level operations supporting millions of clients.

The essential elements of a cloud service deployment are given above. In order to develop enterprise-wide applications, a comprehensive viewpoint has to be assumed with deployment models from the following list: (Mel op cit.)

> *Private cloud.* The cloud infrastructure is operated solely for an organization. It may be managed by the organization or a third party and may exist on premise or off-premise.

> *Community cloud.* The cloud infrastructure is shared by several organizations and supports a specific community that has shared concerns (e.g., mission, security requirements, policy, and compliance considerations). It may be managed by the organizations or a third party and may exist on-premises or off-premises.

> *Public cloud.* The cloud infrastructure is made available to the general public or a large industry group and is owned by an organization selling cloud services.

> *Hybrid cloud.* The cloud infrastructure is a composition of two or more clouds (private, community, or

public) that remain unique entities but are bound together by standardized or proprietary technology that enables data and application portability (e.g., cloud bursting for load-balancing between clouds).

Many cloud software service application domains will be synthesized from a combination of the deployment models.

CLOUD SERVICE ECONOMICS

Cloud services mark a milestone in IT service provisioning. The cloud model promotes availability and operates through a large ecosystem of different approaches to on-demand accessibility supplied by vendors and various market niches. The pool of shared resources essentially determines the economics of the cloud paradigm.

Cloud service democratization refers to either of three distinct but related forms. In the first instance, known as the availability model, it is the process of making a premium cloud service available for general use, rather than through proprietary services. In the second instance, known as the sharing model, it is the capability of sharing data, infrastructure, and storage that would not be otherwise accessible with on-premises facilities. The final instance, known as the voting model, is the phenomena of giving power to the end user by providing access to facilities that are implicitly more preferable than other cloud resources by virtue of the fact that they are used or referenced more frequently by other end users.

The *availability model* reflects the ability of having access to information, software, and computing resource infrastructure without necessarily having to own it. In many cases, the cost and time elements are too high for many organizations, because the up-front costs and time to develop the information, software, and on-premises resources is simply too great for many potential clients and ISVs. The cost of providing computing infrastructure and software by traditional ISVs is such that it is affordable only by larger businesses. This situation leaves out the long tail of small to medium-sized businesses that could benefit from the solution, if the cost were lower. By lowering the cost of service provisioning by utilizing multi-tenancy technology and taking advantage of economy of scale achieved through multiple clients from the cloud, business software services are available to the long-tail market.

The *sharing model* refers to the fact that three major classes of technical resources are available, on a shared basis, through the cloud platforms: data and information, infrastructure services, and data storage facilities. In the case of *data and information*, content can be shared between users from the same client, between clients, and between platforms from the same user. Effectively, more information is available to more users. *Infrastructure sharing* is a major category of cloud service and is a major cost to an IT shop. It includes software, hardware, and security services. With software, comprehensive facilities are available at a lower price, because the cost is shared among thousands of users. With hardware, the end user does not need to plan for peak periods and growth, since elasticity is designed into the architecture of cloud platforms. This is the "scalability" characteristic of utility services. For security, federated security systems are shared among users and clients enabling mobility between diverse computing platforms. *Data storage sharing* refers to the common habitation of data on a cloud platform by several clients. Storage multiplicity, commonly available on cloud platforms, reduces organizational concerns in the general area of disaster planning.

The value of certain services, such as web auctions (e.g., e-Bay), user-supported encyclopedias (e.g., Wiki), and modern search engines (e.g., Google), is derived from the fact that many people use them. This is known as the *voting model*. The power of such facilities lies in the fact that each individual user votes by choosing to use the respective service. With a web auction, it is the interchange between users that gives the facility its democratic power. With an updatable online encyclopedia, an individual end user has the power of updating an entry. This option allows the informational resource to evolve as more people use it. With a search engine, such as Google, it is the method of page ranking, wherein the number of page references to an object page gives its score, and allows a universe of users to democratize a page. Collectively, cloud service democratization essentially enables the delivery of computing service to more clients at a reduced cost.

The basis for the monetization of cloud computing is software-as-a-service (SaaS), commonly regarded as software hosted service from a cloud platform. The varieties of software-as-a-service are non-configurable, single-tenant, and multi-tenant. With *non-configurable SaaS*, the service provider delivers a unique set of features that are hosted in the cloud through a cloud platform and Internet accessibility to the client. With *single-tenant SaaS*, the client has isolated access to a common set of features, perhaps configured in a distinctive way. With *multi-tenant SaaS*, the provider hosts common program logic and unique data elements for multiple clients on scalable infrastructure resources supported via a cloud platform.

BUSINESS AND SERVICE MODELS

The salient features of the cloud computing business model are summarized as follows:

- The ownership of the software is transferred to the cloud service provider.
- The responsibility for hardware, application software, storage facilities, and professional services resides with the provider.
- Systems software is available from a trusted vendor for supporting cloud services.
- Data centers are available for sustaining the operational structure and supporting the requisite fabric needed to utilize server farms.

Accordingly, the business model provides the economy of scale needed to target the long tail by providers and reduces up-front and operational costs for the client.

The SaaS provider with cloud computing will characteristically experience high up-front costs for infrastructure and software development. The SaaS client will have to give up a certain level of control to benefit from the economy-of-scale supplied by the provider. There are lingering questions over "who owns the software," "who owns the data," and information security.

The cloud service models give an ontological view of what a cloud service is. A cloud service system is a set of elements that facilitate the development of cloud applications. Here is a description of the three layers in the NIST service model description: (Mel op cit.)

> *Cloud Software as a Service (SaaS).* The capability provided to the consumer is the use of the provider's applications running on a cloud infrastructure. The applications are accessible from various client devices through a thin client interface such as a web browser (e.g., web-based email). The consumer does not manage or control the underlying cloud infrastructure including network, servers, operating systems, storage, or even individual application capabilities, with the possible exception of limited user-specific application configuration settings.

> *Cloud Platform as a Service (PaaS).* The capability provided to the consumer is that of deploying onto the cloud infrastructure consumer-created or acquired applications developed through the use of programming languages and tools supported by the provider. The consumer does not manage or control the underlying cloud infrastructure including network, servers, operating systems, or storage, but has control over the deployed applications and possibly application hosting environment configurations.

Cloud Infrastructure as a Service (IaaS). The capability provided to the consumer is the capability of provisioning processing, storage, networks, and other fundamental computing resources where the consumer is able to deploy and run arbitrary software, which can include operating systems and applications. The consumer does not manage or control the underlying cloud infrastructure but has control over the operating system, storage, and deployed applications, as well as limited control over selected networking components (e.g., host firewalls).

The three service model elements should be deployed in a cloud environment with the essential characteristics in order to achieve a cloud status

QUICK SUMMARY

1. Cloud computing is a means of accessing computer facilities via the Internet. (The *cloud* is a metaphor for the Internet.)
2. Cloud service facilities are characterized by four key factors: necessity, reliability, usability, and scalability.
3. Software-as-a-service (SaaS) is software deployed as a hosted service and accessed over the Internet.
4. For the cloud client, business service is a balance between control and economy of scale.
5. A cloud platform is based on an operating system that runs in the cloud and provides an infrastructure for software development and deployment.
6. Cloud service *democratization* refers to information and computing availability, information sharing, and the exercise of user preference in supplying information service.

7.   Cloud service *monetization* refers to gaining financial benefit through cloud access and economy-of-scale for both provider and client.

REFERENCES AND SELECTED READING

1   Anderson, C. 2006. *The Long Tail*. New York: Hyperion.
2   Cloud Computing: The Evolution of Software-as-a-Science. 2008. *Arizona State University W.P. Carey School of Business*, June 4, 2008, knowledge.wpcarey.asu.edu.
3   Cavoukian, A. 2009. *Privacy in the Clouds*. Toronto: Information and Privacy Commission of Ontario (www.ipc.on.ca).
4   Chappell, D. 2008 A Short Introduction to Cloud Platforms. *Microsoft Corporation*.
5   Chong, F. and G. Carraro. 2006. Architecture Strategies for Catching the Long Tail. *Microsoft Corporation*.
6   Chong, F. 2008. Application Marketplaces and the Money Trail. *Microsoft Corporation*.
7   IBM Corporation. 2009. The Benefits of Cloud Computing. Form DW03004-USEN-00.
8   Katzan, H. 2009. Cloud Software Service: Concepts, Technology, Economics. *Service Science*, 1(4):256-269.
9   Martin, R and J. Hoover. 2008. Guide to Cloud Computing. *Information Week*, June 21, 2008, www.informationweek.com.
10   Mell, P. and T. Grance. 2009a. The NIST Definition of Cloud Computing. National Institute of Standards and Technology, Information Technology Laboratory, Version 15, 10-7-09. (http://www.csrc.nist.gov/groups/SNS/cloud-computing/index.html)
11   Mell, P., Badger, L., and T. Grance. 2009b. Effectively and Securely Using the Cloud Computing Paradigm. National Institute of Standards and Technology, Information Technology Laboratory, 10-7-09. (http://www.csrc.nist.gov/groups/SNS/cloud-computing/index.html)
12   Miller, M. 2008. Cloud Computing: Web-Based Applications That Change the Way You Work and Collaborate Online, Indianapolis: Que Publishing.
13   Rappa, M. 2004. The utility business model and the future of computing services. *IBM Systems Journal*, 43(1):32-41.
14   Reese, G. 2009. *Cloud Application Architectures: Building Applications and Infrastructure in the Cloud*, Sebastopol, CA: O'Reilly Media, Inc.

6

CLOUD COMPUTING ECONOMICS: DEMOCRATIZATION AND MONETIZATION OF SERVICES

INTRODUCTION

The discipline of modern information systems is based on service science, and within that domain, this paper seeks to analyze the underlying principles that govern the exchangeable value of cloud computer services. Throughout, we will attempt to show the real value of cloud service, the different parts of which a cloud service is constructed, and the forces that govern the dynamics of service value. In fact, if one replaces the concept of labor with that of service, the principles of service science can be derived from the essential work of Adam Smith [20], most pointedly in his notions of "value in use" and "value in exchange." One of the defining characteristics of cloud computing is the transfer of control from the client domain to the cloud service provider. Another is that the client benefits from economy of scale on the part of the provider. There are differences of opinion on exactly what cloud computing is, and this paper attempts to mediate the various economic positions.

BASIC CLOUD COMPUTING CONCEPTS

Cloud computing is a means of accessing computer facilities via the Internet, where the adjective "cloud" reflects the diagrammatic use of a cloud as a metaphor for the Internet. Most of us have been using cloud-computing facilities in one form or another for years through ordinary email and the World Wide Web. Recently, the term has come to reflect the use of software and the running of computer applications via the Internet where the computer infrastructure and software are not "on premises." Cloud computing, as a form of service provisioning, has given rise to several related concepts, such as mesh computing, cloud platforms, and software plus service.

Conceptualization

A proper, but not necessarily definitive, conceptualization of cloud computing is to use office-class applications via your web browser over the Internet instead of having those applications reside on your "on premises" computer. In this instance, the service provider supplies the network access, security, application software, and data storage from a data center located somewhere on the Internet and implemented as a form of server farm with the requisite infrastructure. A service would have ubiquitous access through a web browser or mobile device. In general, the cloud computing concept is not limited to single-function applications, such as those available with typical office suites, but could include comprehensive enterprise applications pieced together from components residing in varying Internet locations.

Utility Computing

Every year organizations spend millions of dollars on their IT infrastructure consisting of hardware, system software, applications, networks, people, and other organizational assets. With "on demand" computing, they can plug into the wall, figuratively speaking, and only pay for the IT services they use. The general concept is called *utility computing* that is accessed as most public utilities. When appropriate, a service utility is a viable option for obtaining computing services, the essence of which is in the packaging of computer services as a metered facility without up-front costs for IT infrastructure. In the current view of things, a services utility is network based and is dependant upon the Internet as a transport mechanism. In recent years, computing has become the operational medium for business, government, education, and a part of everyday life for most people, and as with electric utilities, computing utilities have evolved from being a luxury to an everyday necessity.

Cloud Service Characteristics

Cloud service utilities are characterized by four key factors: necessity, reliability, usability, and scalability. *Necessity* refers to the idea that a preponderance of users depend on the utility to satisfy everyday needs. *Reliability* refers to the expectation that the utility will be available when the user requires it. *Usability* refers to the requirement that the utility is easy and convenient to use – regardless of the complexity of the underlying infrastructure. *Scalability* refers to the fact that the utility has sufficient capacity to allow the users to experience the benefits of an expandable utility that provides economy of scale. Certainly, modern Internet facilities for search operations that engage thousands of servers satisfy these characteristics.

The notion of "paying for what one uses" is a compelling argument for using the cloud for special or all computing needs. The proof of the pudding may be in the details. The key question is whether the service should be based on a metered model or a subscription model. With the *metered model*, the usage is easily measured, monitored, and verified and lends itself to managerial control on the part of the user. In addition, metering can be applied to differing levels of service. With the *subscription model*, usage is difficult to control and monitor and its adoption is favored by managers more concerned with convenience than with resource control.

The difference between application services and multi-tenant services may very well be the deciding factor in determining whether metered or subscriber service is the way to go. With *multi-tenant service*, several clients may share the same software with separate data – as in the case of office processing. With *application service*, the service provider supplies one instance of the software per client, thereby lending itself to a form of metered service. In the latter case, the notion of a client should be regarded as an environment comprised of several users.

Hosting And Virtualization

A common example of utility computing is *hosting*, wherein an application service provides "off premises" computer services on a subscription or pay-as-you-go basis. The practice is prevalent among relatively small software developers that require expensive computer facilities. A service provider usually supplies requisite services on a time-sharing basis through communications facilities, and the service provided is the access to and utilization of a computing platform comprised of a computer system, an operating system, and necessary utility facilities. This is the origin of the *Platform as a Service* (PaaS) concept, often sustained through virtualization.

Virtualization refers to the provisioning of a "not real but virtual" computing environment created through a software facility known as a *hypervisor* with the capability of managing several diverse computing platforms, executing concurrently, so that the client is given the operational advantage and illusion of having a unique copy of the selected platform. The hypervisor controls the underlying computer hardware and software and passes control to a specific client instance on a demand basis [12].

Business Aspects of Cloud Services

The long tail [8] is a conceptualization of the unique business opportunities available through Internet access, exemplified by online book sellers and software services. A brick-and-mortar bookseller has a limited amount of self space and typically stocks only the most popular books. Online booksellers do not have the same limitation and are able to take advantage of the long tail, as suggested by Figure 1, to provide opportunities not available otherwise. The long-tail phenomenon also applies to line-of-business software and consumer-oriented services to provide a level of economy of scale not otherwise available with "on premises" software and the requisite computing platforms. The long-tail perspective provides a basis for the democratization and monetization of cloud computing. Because the application software with cloud computing is not executed on a local computer, it is useful for connecting people and organizations in various combinations across the Web and supporting mobile computing. Cloud computing should not be confused with outsourcing. With outsourcing, an existing function is moved out of the department, enterprise, or geographic jurisdiction. With cloud computing service, the home of an application originates in the cloud.

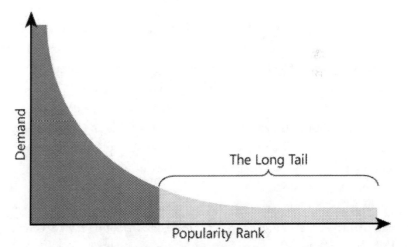

Figure 1. The long-tail concept. (Chong and Carraro [8], p. 8)

It is difficult to state the difference between cloud computing and utility computing, because they both appear to refer to the same phenomena. Digging a little deeper, however, it would appear that utility computing is more of a business concept – perhaps a business model – providing "pay for what you get" services, where the operational framework could be traditional batch processing, local networks, enterprise networks, or the Internet. In fact, utility computing has the flavor of a "spin off" of a non-core service to another organizational entity – either internally or externally. In general, utility computing could use the Internet, but that is not a defining characteristic.

Cloud computing, on the other hand, is by definition an Internet-based facility, with the Internet providing the accessibility component. Service clients do not typically own the hardware and software infrastructure, so a major advantage of cloud computing from the client's perspective is the availability of software, storage, and computing resources without up-front infrastructure costs.

BUSINESS AND CONSUMER SERVICES

Chong and Carraro [8] define software-as-a-service (SaaS) as software deployed as a hosted service and accessed over the Internet. The key features of SaaS are where the programs reside and how they are accessed. The two kinds of software in this category are business software and consumer software. Business software provides business services and emphasizes business solutions, such as CRM, SCM, ERP, and human resources. Consumer software provides personal solutions, such as office applications, that are often available at no cost in their cloud versions.

With business services, the most important consideration is whether the process is executed in-house or as a cloud service. When the process is handled in-house, total control over the operation is obtained along with limited opportunity for achieving economy-of-scale. As processes are distributed outward on the cloud, control is decreased but opportunities for achieving economy-of-scale are increased. The considerations are different with consumer services. Pure service, as with office applications, provides practically no control over the application to the client and a reasonably high-level of economy-of-scale to the provider. In many cases, consumer services are advertising supported and are complimentary to the client through advertising. In addition to the metered and subscription models, the advertising-supported model is another means of monetizing cloud computing.

Business applications that reside "on premises" are governed by the traditional considerations of application acquisition and deployment. If an application resides on and is deployed from the cloud, then two options exist:

1. Build the software yourself (or have it built for you) and run it on the cloud as a hosted service – perhaps using a cloud platform.
2. Obtain the application software from an independent software vendor (ISV) and run it on the cloud in a standard or modified mode.

In the former case, all users access the same version of the software. In the latter case, a client gets a customized version achieved with a separate code base, or its equivalent, configuration options, or operational metadata. The subject of business services is covered in more detail in a subsequent section.

The primary advantage of a cloud consumer service is that it is typically free to the client, as well as being accessible from any location via the Internet, and it yields advertising-supported revenue for the provider. Consumer services have a near-zero marginal cost of distribution to clients, because of the long tail, and require only a fraction of the number of clients to respond to advertising. This is the well-known *Freemium Business Model* [1], characterized as follows: In the free sample product model, you give away 1% of your product to sell the additional 99%, whereas in the freemium model, you give away 99% to sell 1%. Because of the scale of the Internet with millions of users, you can reach a large market, so that the 1% is a huge amount.

Software plus Service (S+S) refers to a user-centric approach to service deployment by combining "on premises" computing (fat client) with enhanced services on the cloud. The enhanced services combine advanced functionality with the capability to scale up to meet peak computing demands for both business and consumer services. A related feature of S+S involves the distribution of service pack software updates for both system and application software and the provisioning of automatic software downloading.

Clearly, the business model for the deployment of both SaaS and S+S changes with the adoption of cloud computing. The ownership of software shifts from the client to the provider, along with the responsibility for the technology infrastructure and its management [8]. The marketing targets for SaaS and S+S clients are service consumers and small to medium-sized businesses, and economy of scale is achieved through specialization and the development of cloud platforms.

CLOUD SERVICE ARCHITECTURE

A comprehensive SaaS application structure includes a continuum of architectural levels, based on the capability of handling multiple clients and software configurability. Four levels are identified. The number of levels in any specific operational environment is based on the cloud platform and its characteristics.

> **Level One.** At the first level, the users within a client domain address a single instance of an application running on a server. Each client/instance is totally independent of other client/instances running on the same server. This is the traditional hosted service operating in the cloud. Each software instance is individually customized for each client.

Level Two. At the second level, the server hosts a separate instance of the software for each client, but the instance is a configurable version of the same code base, reducing maintenance costs and contributing to increased economy-of-scale.

Level Three. At the third architectural level, the vendor runs a sole instance that is shared by multiple clients. The feature set for each client is determined by configurable metadata, and authorization/ security policies insure the separation of user data.

Level Four. At the fourth level, the same "level three" instances are run on a server farm with fabric for lead balancing.

The choice among architectural levels is determined by the provider/client's business, architectural, and operational models.

Cloud Platforms

A *cloud platform* is an operating system that runs in the cloud. More specifically, a cloud platform provides services to applications in the same manner that "software as a service" programs provide services to clients. Both use the Internet as a transport medium. A cloud platform resides in a cloud data center and exists as a powerful computing facility, a storage system, an advanced operating system, support software, and the necessary fabric to sustain a server farm and scale up to support millions of Internet clients. A cloud platform is as much about operating in the cloud, as it is about developing applications for the cloud. A cloud platform provides the facility for an application developer to create applications that run in the cloud; and in so doing, the application developer uses services that are available from the cloud. Chappell [6, 7] lists three kinds of cloud services:

SaaS user services, on-premises application development services (attached services), and cloud application development services. An *SaaS application* runs entirely in the cloud and is accessible through the Internet from an on-premises browser or mobile device. *Attached services* provide functionality through the cloud to support service-oriented architecture (SOA) type component development that runs on-premises. *Cloud application development services* support the development of applications that typically interact while running in the cloud and on-premises.

A cloud platform can be conceptualized as being comprised of three complementary groups of services: foundations, infrastructure services, and application services. The *foundation* refers to the operating system, storage system, file system, and database system. *Infrastructure services* include authorization/authentication/security facilities, integration between infrastructure and application services, and online storage facilities. *Application services* refer to ordinary business services that expose "functional" services as SOA components. Cloud platforms are a lot like enterprise-level platforms, except that they are designed to scale up to Internet-level operations supporting millions of clients.

Application Services

Application services are designed to be used by people, and infrastructure services are designed to be used by applications. The basic idea of cloud platforms is that SaaS applications will be created by developers to provide services used by people, and will use cloud infrastructure services. *Software plus service* (S+S) is an in-between point in the cloud service continuum, falling between the pure-play user-centric set of services and the large-scale enterprise application systems in which on-premises and cloud software interact to support comprehensive business services. In the S+S hierarchy, the cloud platform should consist of building block, attached, and finished services to complement application services, mentioned previously, and to support a flexible set of operational scenarios that include PCs, Web access, mobile devices, on-premises servers, and cloud-based services [11].

DEMOCRATIZATION OF CLOUD SERVICES

The origin of democratization from a cloud computing perspective lies in the fact that people can have better access to software, computing facilities, and data through network effects, by employing cloud computing facilities rather than strictly using "on premises" software and hosting. Essentially this means a person or an organization can obtain results via the Internet previously available only to the privileged few. The topics of business intelligence (BI) and knowledge management (KM) represent good examples. In banking, for example, a snapshot of a customer's profile from various data sources would heretofore require the development of special computer programs. With cloud computing and democratization, that same information could be obtained dynamically and presented through an adaptable dashboard, enhancing collaborative efforts and business agility.

Overview

Cloud service democratization refers to either of three distinct but related forms. In the first instance, known as the availability model, it is the process of making a premium cloud service available for general use, rather than through proprietary services. In the second instance, known as the sharing model, it is the capability of sharing data, infrastructure, and storage that would not be otherwise accessible with on-premises facilities. The final instance, known as the voting model, is the phenomena of giving power to the end user by providing access to facilities that are implicitly more preferable than other cloud resources by virtue of the fact that they are used or referenced more frequently by other end users.

Availability Model

The *availability model* reflects the ability of having access to information, software, and computing resource infrastructure without necessarily having to own it. In many cases, the cost and time elements are too great for many organizations, because the up-front costs and time to develop the information, software, and on-premises resources is simply too great for many potential clients and ISVs. Figure 2 represents the availability situation for business users. The cost of providing computing infrastructure and software by traditional ISVs is such that it is affordable only to larger businesses. This situation leaves out the long tail of small to medium-sized businesses that could benefit from the solution if the cost were lower.

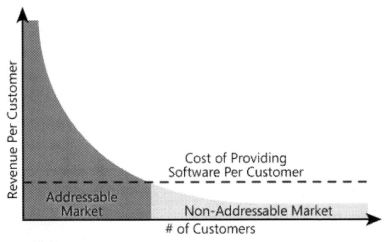

Figure 2. The long-tail market concept for traditional ISVs. (Chong and Carraro [8], p. 29)

By lowering the cost of service provisioning by utilizing multi-tenancy technology and taking advantage of economy of scale achieved through multiple clients from the cloud, business software services are available to the long-tail market, as suggested in Figure 3.

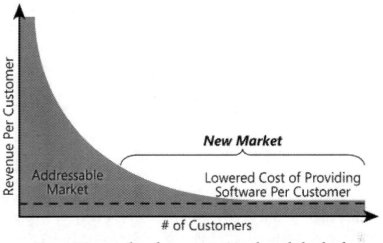

Figure 3. Long-tail market opportunities through the cloud and software services. (Chong and Carraro [8], p. 30)

Sharing Model

The *sharing model* refers to the fact that three major classes of technical resources are available on a shared basis through the availability of cloud platforms: data and information, infrastructure services, and data storage facilities. In the case of *data and information*, content can be shared between users from the same client, between clients, and between platforms from the same user. Effectively, more information is available to more users.

Infrastructure sharing is a major category and a major cost to an IT shop. It includes software, hardware, and security services. With software, comprehensive facilities are available at a lower price, because the cost is shared among thousands of users. With hardware, the end user need not have to plan for peak periods and growth, since elasticity is designed into the architecture of cloud platforms. This is the "scalability" characteristic of utility services. With security, federated security systems are shared among users and clients enabling mobility between diverse computing platforms.

Data storage sharing refers to the common habitation of data on a cloud platform by several clients. Storage multiplicity, commonly available on cloud platforms, reduces organizational concerns in the general area of disaster planning.

Voting Model

The value of certain services, such as web auctions (e.g., e-Bay), user-supported encyclopedias (e.g., Wiki), and modern search engines (e.g., Google), is derived from the fact that many people use them. The power of such facilities lies in the fact that each individual user votes by choosing to use the respective service. With a web auction, it is the interchange between users that gives the facility its democratic power. With an updatable online encyclopedia, an individual end user has the power of updating an entry. This option allows the informational resource to evolve as more people use it. With a search engine, such as Google, it is the method of page ranking, wherein the number of page references to an object page gives its score, and allows a universe of users to democratize a page.

Collectively, cloud service democratization essentially enables the delivery of computing service to more clients at a reduced cost. This topic is introduced in the next section.

MONETIZATION OF CLOUD SERVICES

The basis for the monetization of cloud computing is software-as-a-service (SaaS), commonly regarded as software hosted service from a cloud platform. The varieties of software-as-a-service are non-configurable, single- tenant, and multi-tenant. With *non-configurable SaaS*, the service provider delivers a unique set of features that are hosted in the cloud through a cloud platform and Internet accessibility to the client. With *single-tenant SaaS*, the client has isolated access to a common set of features, perhaps configured in a distinctive way. With *multi-tenant SaaS*, the provider hosts common program logic and unique data elements for multiple clients on scalable infrastructure resources supported via a cloud platform.

Application Domain

The application domain of cloud computing, introduced earlier under "Cloud Service Characteristics," is usually divided into two diverse groups: business services and consumer services. The emphasis with service monetization is on business services, since the client and the independent software vendor (ISV) would have some control over the business model, whereas with consumer services, the freemium model monopolizes the service landscape. In either case, the major considerations involved with the development of cloud applications are multi-customization, extensibility, isolation, and cloud storage, known as data scaling.

Business Model

The business model for cloud computing reflects how service providers can increase revenue and how clients can reduce operational costs of services over on-premises facilities. There are two areas that can be addressed: the application architecture and the operational structure. From a monetization viewpoint, there are two options for application architecture: common features and unique features. For operational structure, the options are single-tenant and multi-tenant. The various options are regarded as service drivers and are summarized in Figure 4.

TENANCY

	Single	Multiple
Common	Software cost low Operational cost high	Software cost low Operational cost low
Unique	Software cost high Operational cost high	Software cost high Operational cost low

(left axis label: **FEATURES**)

Figure 4. Service Drivers for Cloud Service Monetization.

The salient features of the cloud computing business model are summarized as follows:

- The ownership of the software is transferred to the cloud service provider.
- The responsibility for hardware, application software, storage facilities, and professional services resides with the provider.
- Systems software is available from a trusted vendor for supporting cloud services.
- Data centers are available for sustaining the operational structure and supporting the requisite fabric needed to utilize service farms.

Accordingly, the business model provides the economy of scale needed to target the long tail by providers and reducing up-front and operational costs for the client.

The SaaS provider with cloud computing will characteristically experience high up-front costs for infrastructure and software development. This is covered later. The SaaS client will have to give up a certain level of control to benefit from the economy-of-scale supplied by the provider. There are lingering questions over "who owns the software," "who owns the data," and information security.

Client Perspective

The client perspective with SaaS, and essentially all of cloud computing, involves features provided by application and systems software, service-level agreements, and price. How the software is designed and deployed in the cloud is a provider consideration. Any technical decisions made by the provider as to adopting non-configurable, single-tenant, or multi-tenant services are reflected in the user's price and service-level agreement.

It is now possible to be specific about service monetization for software utilization, and the various options are reflected in four categories: perpetual license, subscription, transaction based, and ad funded [5].

Perpetual license refers to an "up front" payment for service, and unlimited access for an unlimited time. The is an attractive form for seller and buyer, since customer churn is reduced and utilization need not be a monetization concern. Effectively, the financial considerations and technical issues are essentially separated. When considering cloud versus on-premises hosting, the cards are definitely in favor of the client, even though the provider can always attach monetization schemes such as maintenance fees under the guise of software upgrades.

Subscription, as a form of cloud service monetization, can be conceptualized as a time-based perpetual license, often applied to multiple users. In the modern view of software acquisition, an individual buyer purchases only the right to use the software. When applied to organizations, the subscription method provides a reduced rate to multiple users along with a time-dependent renewal fee.

Transaction based monetization requires a close association between hosting software and financial billing. This form of pricing allows the provider with a means of recouping its up-front infrastructure costs, while permitting the client to benefit from economy-of-scale. This form of monetization requires a level of trust between client and provider and experiences certain "no repudiation" issues. As with telephone service, monthly plans are often preferable to pay-as-you-go plans.

Ad funded monetization schemes appear to be most popular with consumer services as described with the freemium mode offered previously. The software service is provided for free and a sponsor pays the cost in return for the consumer's attention. A related form is *Software plus Service* (S+S), wherein the provider supplies access to enhanced features at a fee to support the basic consumer service.

Business Perspective

An element of software is essentially a collection of features – functions that perform a computational task. The set of features in a product or service support the selling aspects of that item. The cost of providing software services in a cloud environment are substantial and involve design, implementation, testing, marketing, and support activities. In short, complex software has a higher cost over simple software. When cloud software is architected for multi-tenancy to achieve sharing and economy-of-scale for the client, the costs are dramatically higher. Cloud software provisioning is a trade-off between features and tenancy. Each of the items, i.e., features and tenancy, is actually a continuum, even though it is customarily treated as "lower" and "higher" to simplify the analysis and understanding. The scenario is inherent in the graphs in Figure 4.

Cost per tenant is the cost of delivering an element of software to one client and covers any requisite expenses needed for the associated service. Multi-tenant architecture maximizes sharing between users and increases the total revenue and economy of scale for the client; however, it increases development costs.

Cost per feature is the cost of implementing a specific functionality. Simpler features cost less to develop and maintain. Adding multi-tenancy increases the cost of a feature. The tenancy/feature conundrum is summarized as follows: "... multi-tenancy incurs a higher cost per feature, but lower cost per tenant while isolation has lower cost per feature but higher cost per tenant."[5] Figure 5 summarizes in graphical form the advantages of each approach over time. As the tenant base grows (t3 in the diagram), multi-tenancy has good monetization for the provider.

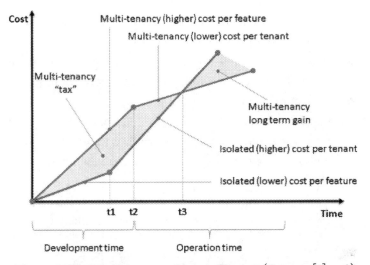

Figure 5. Cost per Feature vs. Cost per Tenant. (Carraro [5], p. 2)

A promising approach to achieving economy-of-scale is to use virtualization at the cloud platform operating system level instead of designing an application for multi-tenancy.

QUICK SUMMARY

1. The disciplines of information systems and cloud computing are based on service science.
2. The principles of service science can be derived from the essential work of Adam Smith in the areas of "value in use" and "value in exchange."

3. Cloud computing is a means of accessing computer facilities via the Internet. (The *cloud* is a metaphor for the Internet.)
4. Cloud service utilities are characterized by four key factors: necessity, reliability, usability, and scalability.
5. The long tail is a conceptualization of business opportunities available through Internet access.
6. Software as a service (SaaS) is software deployed as a hosted service and accessed over the Internet.
7. For the cloud client, business service is a balance between control and economy of scale.
8. A cloud platform is based on an operating system that runs in the cloud and provides an infrastructure for software development and deployment.
9. Cloud service *democratization* refers to ubiquitous information and computing availability, information sharing, and the exercise of user preference in supplying information service.
10. Cloud service *monetization* refers to gaining financial benefit through cloud access for both provider and client.

REFERENCES

1 Anderson, C. 2004. The Long Tail. *Wired Blog Network.*
2 Cloud Computing: The Evolution of Software-as-a-Science. *Arizona State University W.P. Carey School of Business,* June 4, 2008, knowledge.wpcarey. asu.edu, (2008).
3 Carraro, G. 2007. Cost per feature vs. cost per tenant. *Microsoft Corporation,* blogs.msdn.com/gianpaolo/archive.
4 Carraro, G. 2008. I don't believe we are still talking about whether SaaS = multi-tenancy … . *Microsoft Corporation,* blogs.msdn.com/gianpaolo/ archive.
5 Carraro, G. 2008. Monetization: the next frontier of SaaS/S+S architecture. *Microsoft Corporation,* blogs.msdn.com/gianpaolo/archive.
6 Chappell, D. 2008. A Short Introduction to Cloud Platforms. *Microsoft Corporation.*

7   Chappell, D. 2008. Introducing the Azure Services Platform. *Microsoft Corporation.*

8   Chong, F. and G. Carraro. 2006. Architecture Strategies for Catching the Long Tail. *Microsoft Corporation.*

9   Chong, F. 2008. Application Marketplaces and the Money Trail. *Microsoft Corporation.*

10 Utility Based Cloud Power. *Computers Journal,* February 12, 2009, www.dirjournal.com, (2009).

11 Foley, M. 2008. *Microsoft 2.0,* Indianapolis: Wiley Publishing, Inc.

12 Katzan, H. 1986. *Operating Systems: A Pragmatic Approach (2e).* Hoboken, NJ: John Wiley and Sons.

13 Katzan, H. 2008. Cloud Computing, I-Service, and IT Service Provisioning. *Journal of Service Science,* 1(2):57-64.

14 Katzan, H. 2008. *Service Science: Concepts, Technology, Management,* New York: iUniverse, Inc.

15 Knorr, E and G. Gruman. 2008. What cloud computing really means. *InfoWorld,* April 07, 2008, www.infoworld.com.

16 Martin, R and J. Hoover . 2008. Guide to Cloud Computing. *Information Week,* June 21, 2008, www.informationweek.com.

17 Miller, M. 2008. *Cloud Computing: Web-Based Applications That Change the Way You Work and Collaborate Online,* Indianapolis: Que Publishing.

18 Rappa, M. 2004. The utility business model and the future of computing services. *IBM Systems Journal,* 43(1):xx-xx.

19 Perry, G. 2008., How Cloud & Utility Computing are Different. *GigaSpace Technologies,* February 28, 2008, www.gigacom.com.

20 Smith, Adam. 1776. *The Wealth of Nations,* published as "An Inquiry Into the Nature and Causes of the Wealth of Nations" in London, England.

21 Wikipedia. 2008. Software as a Service. www.wikipedia.com.

7

ONTOLOGICAL VIEW OF CLOUD COMPUTING

CLOUD COMPUTING CONCEPTS

Cloud computing is a means of providing computer facilities via the Internet, but that is only half of the picture. The other half is that it is also a means of accessing those same computer facilities via the Internet from different locations. When a large bank, for example, moves to cloud computing for online operations, it necessarily considers both halves of the equation. The adjective "cloud" reflects the diagrammatic use of a cloud as a metaphor for the Internet. In telecommunications, a *cloud* is the unpredictable part of a network through which business and personal information passes from end-to-end and over which we do not have direct knowledge or control.[8] Most of us have been using cloud-computing facilities in one form or another for years through ordinary email and the World Wide Web. Recently, the term has come to reflect the use of software and the running of computer applications via the Internet where the computer infrastructure and software are not "on premises."

Cloud computing is an evolving concept, even though major financial institutions, consulting organizations, and software vendors have invested heavily in the technology and associated business practices, and the U.S.

---

[8] See *Privacy in the Clouds* by Cavoukin for more information on this subject.

Government has endorsed the model for federal computer operations. Surprisingly, there are few papers in the academic/professional literature on the subject, leading to divergent views on what the cloud-computing paradigm actually represents. The National Institute of Standards and Technology has stepped into the fray, and this paper essentially covers a *public domain*[9] definition of the topic. (Mel 2009a, Mel 2009b) In this paper, we will be concerned with concepts and terminology.

CLOUD COMPUTING UTILITY

In principle, all utilities are the same and characterized by four key factors: necessity, reliability, usability, and scalability. *Necessity* refers to the notion of a preponderance of users depending on the utility to satisfy everyday needs. *Reliability* refers to the expectation that the utility will be available when the user requires it. *Usability* refers to the requirement that the utility is easy and convenient to use – regardless of the complexity of the underlying infrastructure. *Scalability* refers to the fact that the utility has sufficient capacity to allow the users to experience the benefits of an expandable utility that provides economy of scale. (Rappa 2004) Certainly, modern Internet facilities for search operations that engage thousands of servers satisfy these characteristics, and one would expect cloud services to do the same. (Katzan 2009) Cloud computing is different from a conventional utility because it deals with information and computers that may contain sensitive information leading to considerations of security and privacy.

CLOUD ARCHITECTURE

A cloud architecture is a collection of three categories of information resources for achieving business agility, availability,

---

[9] Public domain is an intellectual property designation for content not owned by anyone and usually paid for with taxpayer money. Proper attribution is expected but not required with public domain content.

collaboration, and elasticity in the deployment and use of cloud services that include software, information, and a cloud infrastructure. The *software category* includes system software, application software, infrastructure software, and accessibility software. The *information category* refers to large collections of data and the requisite database and management facilities needed for efficient and secure storage utilization. The *category of cloud infrastructure* includes compute[10] resources, network facilities, and the fabric for scalable consumer operations. We are going to adopt an ontological formulation for the description of a cloud framework that necessarily includes three classes of information: terminology, architectural requirements, and a reference model. The description adopts the National Institute of Standards and Technology (NIST) cloud-computing paradigm. (Mell 2009b, Brunette 2009)

Ontology

Ontology is a specification of "what is." In philosophy, use of the term reflects the study of being (or existence) and describes and delineates a collection of basic categories, and also defines the entities and classes of elements within a category. In service science, ontology is a specification of a conceptualization used to enable knowledge sharing. Since ontology concerns existence, an ontological definition of a subject – perhaps a service category – reflects a materialization of a concept obtained through a shared reality. We are going to adopt Gruber's definition of ontology, as "a set of representational primitives with which to model a domain of knowledge or discourse." (Gruber 2008) Most forms of ontology are expressed in an ontology language and share structural similarities, such as individuals, classes, attributes, relations, function, restrictions, rules, axioms, and events. (Sowa 2000) The components determine whether a specific ontology is a domain ontology or an upper ontology. In a *domain ontology*, a

---

[10] The use of the word compute is correct in this instance and is refers in cloud computing to a facility for computer processing.

specific type would be relevant to a particular category, such as in a consumer or business cloud category. In an *upper ontology*, a type would be applicable to all ontologies in the universe of discourse. In the cloud ontology, presented in the following sections, we are going to be developing an upper ontology for cloud services.

Cloud Characteristics

In a cloud environment, the essential cloud characteristics fall in the former category. The NIST lists the characteristics as: (Mell 2009a)

> *On-demand self-service.* A consumer can unilaterally provision computing capabilities, such as server time and network storage, automatically without requiring human interaction with a service's provider.

> *Broad network access.* Capabilities are available over the network that are accessed through standard mechanisms that promote use by heterogeneous thin or thick client platforms (e.g., mobile phones, laptops, and PDAs).

> *Resource pooling.* The provider's computing resources are pooled to serve multiple consumers using a multi-tenant model, with different physical and virtual resources dynamically assigned and reassigned according to consumer demand. There is a sense of location independence in that the customer generally has no control or knowledge over the exact location of the provided resources but may be able to specify location at a higher level of abstraction (e.g., country, state, or datacenter). Examples of resources include storage, processing, memory, network bandwidth, and virtual machines.

Rapid elasticity. Capabilities can be rapidly and elastically provisioned, in some cases automatically, to quickly scale out and to rapidly be released to quickly scale in. To the consumer, the capabilities available for service provisioning appear to be unlimited and can be obtained in any quantity at any time.

Measured Service. Cloud systems automatically control and optimize resource use by leveraging a metering capability at some level of abstraction appropriate to the type of service (e.g., storage, processing, bandwidth, and active user accounts). Resource usage can be monitored, controlled, and reported providing transparency for both the provider and consumer of the utility service.

The essential characteristics are more than a description of an "application layer." (Youseff 2009) The characteristics give a salient set of reasons why a consumer would want to move to the cloud.

CLOUD SERVICE PROVISIONING

The salient features of the cloud computing business model are summarized as follows:

- The ownership of the software is transferred to the cloud service provider.
- The responsibility for hardware, application software, storage facilities, and professional services resides with the provider.
- Systems software is available from a trusted vendor for supporting cloud services.
- Data centers are available for sustaining the operational structure and for supporting the requisite fabric needed to utilize server farms.

Accordingly, the business model provides the economy of scale needed to target the long tail by providers and reduces up-front and operational costs for the client.

Cloud Application Architecture

A cloud application architecture includes a continuum of service levels, based on the capability of handling multiple clients and software configurations. Two levels are identified here. The number of levels in any specific operational environment is based on the cloud platform and its characteristics.

> **Level One.** At the first level, the server hosts a separate instance of the software for each customer, but the instance is a configurable version of the same code base, reducing maintenance costs and contributing to reduced software costs. This instance is known as *single tenant* software.

> **Level Two.** At the second level, all of the customers within an application client domain address a single instance of an application running on a server. Each client/instance is totally independent of other client/instances running on the same server. Authentication and authorization security policies insure the separation of user data. This instance is known as *multiple tenant* software.

The choice among architectural levels is determined by the provider/client's business, architectural, and operational requirements.

Cloud Platforms

A *cloud platform* is an operating system that runs in the cloud and supports the software-as-a service concept. A cloud platform resides in a cloud data center and exists as a powerful computing facility, a storage system, an advanced operating system, support software, and the necessary fabric to sustain a server farm and scale up to support millions of Internet clients. A cloud platform is as much about operating in the cloud, as it is about developing applications for the cloud. A cloud platform provides the facility for an application developer to create applications that run in the cloud; and, in so doing, the application developer uses services that are available from the cloud. Cloud platforms are a lot like enterprise-level platforms, except that they are designed to scale up to Internet-level operations supporting millions of clients.

A cloud platform can be conceptualized as being comprised of three complementary groups of services: foundations, infrastructure services, and application services. The *foundation* refers to the operating system, storage system, file system, and database system. *Infrastructure services* include authorization/authentication/security facilities, integration between infrastructure and application services, and online storage facilities. *Application services* refer to ordinary business services that expose "functional" services as SOA components. Cloud platforms are a lot like enterprise-level platforms, except that they are designed to scale up to support Internet-level operations.

Service Models

The cloud service models give an ontological view of what a cloud service is. A cloud service system is a set of elements that facilitate the development of cloud applications. (Youseff op cit.) Here is a description of the three layers in the NIST service model description: (Mel op cit.)

> *Cloud Software as a Service (SaaS).* The capability
> provided to the consumer is the use of the provider's
> applications running on a cloud infrastructure.

The applications are accessible from various client devices through a thin client interface such as a web browser (e.g., web-based email). The consumer does not manage or control the underlying cloud infrastructure including network, servers, operating systems, storage, or even individual application capabilities, with the possible exception of limited user-specific application configuration settings.

Cloud Platform as a Service (PaaS). The capability provided to the consumer is that of deploying onto the cloud infrastructure consumer-created or acquired applications developed through the use of programming languages and tools supported by the provider. The consumer does not manage or control the underlying cloud infrastructure including network, servers, operating systems, or storage, but has control over the deployed applications and possibly application hosting environment configurations.

Cloud Infrastructure as a Service (IaaS). The capability provided to the consumer is the capability of provisioning processing, storage, networks, and other fundamental computing resources where the consumer is able to deploy and run arbitrary software, which can include operating systems and applications. The consumer does not manage or control the underlying cloud infrastructure but has control over the operating system, storage, and deployed applications, as well as limited control over selected networking components (e.g., host firewalls).

The three service model elements should be deployed in a cloud environment with the essential characteristics in order to achieve a desired cloud state. Figure 1 gives an idea of how the service models are interrelated.

Service Deployment Models

The essential elements of a cloud service system are given above. In order to develop enterprise-wide applications, a domain ontological viewpoint has to be assumed with deployment models from the following list: (Mel op cit.)

> *Private cloud.* The cloud infrastructure is operated solely for an organization. It can be managed by the organization or a third party and may exist on-premises or off-premises.

> *Community cloud.* The cloud infrastructure is shared by several organizations and supports a specific operational community that has shared concerns (e.g., mission, security requirements, policy, and compliance considerations). It may be managed by an organizations or a third party and may exist on-premises or off-premises.

> *Public cloud.* The cloud infrastructure is made available to the general public or a large industry group and is owned by an organization providing the cloud service.

> *Hybrid cloud.* The cloud infrastructure is a composition of two or more clouds (private, community, or public) that remain unique entities but are bound together by standardized or proprietary technology

that enables data and application portability (e.g., cloud bursting for load-balancing between clouds).

Most cloud software service application domains will be synthesized from a combination of the deployment models.

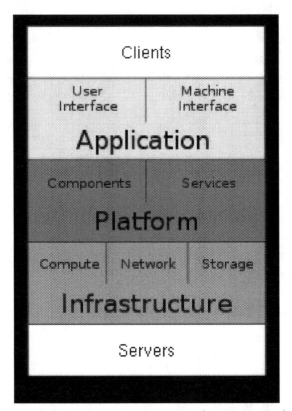

Figure 1. Service Model Architectures. (Wikipedia 2010)

PRIVACY AND SECURITY

Many examples of cloud computing conveniently characterize it as analogous to the electric utility. Historically, the private generators of the twentieth century were replaced by the electricity grids of today. Although similar in some respects, cloud computing is different in one important way. The cloud will typically handle information about which privacy and security are of paramount concern. The key issues therein are identity, accountability, and privacy. The side issues are identity attributes (such as age, gender, and race), accountability (for the security of online activity), and anonymity (in order to protect free speech). The key consideration may turn out to be a matter of control. From an organizational perspective, control over information should remain with the end user. From a personal perspective, the person should have the wherewithal to control his or her identity as well as the release of identity attributes. Who owns the data? Is it the person about whom the data pertains? Is it the organization that prototypically stores its data? Or, is it the cloud provider that physically controls and stores the data somewhere out in cyberspace? As an example, is your financial information (as personal data) your property or is it your bank's business property? They are not rhetorical questions, but issues that must be resolved before moving to a cloud operational environment.

QUICK SUMMARY

1. Cloud computing is a means of accessing computer facilities via the Internet. (The *cloud* is a metaphor for the Internet.)
2. Cloud service facilities are characterized by four key factors: necessity, reliability, usability, and scalability.
3. Software-as-a-service (SaaS) is software deployed as a hosted service and accessed over the Internet.
4. For the cloud client, business service is a balance between control and economy of scale.
5. A cloud platform is based on an operating system that runs in the cloud and provides an infrastructure for software development and deployment.
6. Most cloud software service application domains will be synthesized from a combination of the deployment models.

REFERENCES AND SELECTED READING

1   Anderson, C. 2006. *The Long Tail*. New York: Hyperion.

2   Brunette, G. and R. Mogull (ed). 2009. *Security Guidance for Critical Areas of Focus in Cloud Computing V2.1*. Cloud Security Alliance, December 2009.

3   Cavoukian, A. 2009. *Privacy in the Clouds*. Toronto: Information and Privacy Commission of Ontario (www.ipc.on.ca).

4   Chappell, D. 2008 A Short Introduction to Cloud Platforms. *Microsoft Corporation*.

5   Ferrario, R. and N. Guardino. 2008. Towards an Ontological Foundation for Services Science. *Proceedings of the Future Internet Symposium*, Vienna Austria, 28-30 September 2008.

6   Gruber, T. 2008. Ontology. *Encyclopedia of Database Systems*, Liu, L. and M. Ozsu (Eds.), Springer-Verlag,

7   Katzan, H. 2009. Cloud Computing Economics: Democratization and Monetization of Services. *Journal of Business & Economics Research*, 7(6):1-11.

8   Mell, P. and T. Grance. 2009a. The NIST Definition of Cloud Computing. National Institute of Standards and Technology, Information Technology Laboratory, Version 15, 10-7-09. (http://www.csrc.nist.gov/groups/SNS/cloud-comjputing/index.html)

9   Mell, P., Badger, L., and T. Grance. 2009b. Effectively and Securely Using the Cloud Computing Paradigm. National Institute of Standards and Technology, Information Technology Laboratory, 10-7-09. (http://www.csrc.nist.gov/groups/SNS/cloud-comjputing/index.html)

10 Rappa, M. 2004. The utility business model and the future of computing services. *IBM Systems Journal*, 43(1):32-41.

11 Sowa, J. 2000. *Knowledge Representation: Logical, Philosophical and Computational Foundations*, Brooks Cole Publishing.

12 Wikipedia. 2010. *Cloud Computing*. http://en.wikipedia.org/wiki/Cloud_computing. (Downloaded 01/29/2010).

13 Youseff, L., Butrico, M., and D. Da Silva. 2009. *Toward a Unified Ontology of Cloud Computing*. (Available from the following: (lyouseff@cs.uscb.edu), (butrico@us.ibm.com), and (dilmasilva@us.ibm.com).

8

PRIVACY AS A SERVICE

INTRODUCTION

It has long been recognized that privacy is a two-edged sword, not only for individuals, but also for groups and organizations. Subjects have First and Fourth Amendment rights designed to protect against unwarranted disclosure of information with unlimited scope to unwanted parties without proper authorization by the subject. However, privacy considerations protect criminals and terrorists, in addition to ordinary citizens, groups, and organizations. Protections and other conventions used to safeguard trade secrets can also be employed to enable non-disclosure of design and manufacturing flaws from consumers and regulatory bodies.

Privacy has been in the news for at least forty years originating with Alan Westin's seminal book on the subject entitled *Privacy and Freedom*, published in 1967. Others have joined the struggle, namely (Westin 1977, Miller 1971, Katzan 1980, and Givens 2009) to reference only a few of many, with apologies to those not mentioned. One of the toughest problems facing the computer industry is data protection, summarized very well in 1971 by Arthur R. Miller: (Miller 1971, p.37)

> The new information technologies seem to have given birth to a new social virus – "data-mania." Its symptoms are shortness of breath and heart

palpitations when contemplating a new computer application, a feeling of possessiveness about information and a deep resentment toward those who won't yield it, a delusion that all information handlers can walk on water, and a highly advanced case of astigmatism that prevents the affected victim from perceiving anything but the intrinsic value of data. Fortunately, only some members of the information-handling fraternity have been stricken by the disease.

This quote was written over 39 years ago; what would the author think about today's environment? Based on the concepts implicit in the other papers in this compendium, it would seem that privacy and identity are the two ends of a "personal privacy" continuum, suggested by the following diagram:

Privacy ————————————————— **Identity**

The analogy is not exact but is useful for establishing the notion that the more readily individuals can be identified and their behavior ascertained, the less privacy they possess. The point-of-view adopted in this compendium is that the increased and effective use of mathematical methods together with an increased awareness of key privacy issues can lessen the erosion of personal privacy.

Privacy and Data Protection

Data protection is given the most attention when the privacy of an individual or an organization is jeopardized. According to Alan F. Weston: (Weston 1967)

> Privacy is the claim of individuals, groups, or institutions to determine for themselves when, how, and to what extent information about them is communicated to others.

Privacy is significantly related to data protection because it is an integral part of society and affects the behavior of its members. *Privacy is a service that a subject should expect from and be provided for by society.* The physical state of being private has four primary attributes: solitude, intimacy, anonymity, and reserve, which supply group separation, group participation, group freedom, and personal protection, respectively. These states collectively provide the confidentiality required to participate in a civilized society. Concerns for privacy should be an integral part of a data protection program.

An organization requires privacy to achieve its basic objective – whether it is business, education, or government. The disclosure of private internal affairs affects "brand equity" and is detrimental to success.

Another consideration is personal surveillance – even though it may be socially or legally accepted. When a subject does not have control over its informational profile, there is no safeguard over its authenticity. Therefore, a double barreled approach, consisting of technology and regulation, is required for operating in a global economy. (Katzan, 1980, p. 44)

Information Control

Because of the widespread application of computer and communications technology, there has been a gradual trend among private institutions and government agencies to ignore the individual's need for privacy. Privacy safeguards are the individual's sole line of defense against the exercise of power through information control. Individuals can lose control of information about themselves in three ways:

1. Information obtained against the subject's wishes.
2. Information obtained from an agency against the wishes of the agency and of the subject.
3. Information willingly disclosed by the beneficial user or agency but against the subject's wishes.

Information obtained against a subject's wishes is an area in which privacy is normally expected. This category includes explicit attempts to obtain information and implicit methods where a subject is forced to disclose personal information. Typical actions are:

1. Searches and seizure
2. Compelled self-disclosure
3. Informers and secret agents
4. Participant monitoring
5. Public observation and recording of information
6. Consent for fear of reprisal
7. Disclosure for privilege

Some benefits are commonly associated with disclosure of private information so the fine line between willing and unauthorized disclosure is frequently blurred. In the case of *Information obtained from an agency against the wishes of the agency and of the subject*, the conditions of privacy should apply to the agency as they do to the subject and are normally of concern because of computer security deficiencies and unauthorized access. In the case of *Information willingly disclosed by the beneficial user or agency but against the subject's wishes,* as in interagency transfers, accuracy and context are normally of concern. This is the prototypical *repurposing of information* that lies at the heart of most subjects' concerns over the disclosure of personal information.

Recordkeeping

Records typically fall into four classes: administrative, operational, intelligence, and statistical. In theory, *administrative records* are maintained by governmental agencies and give subjects their identity. For individuals, administrative records normally include birth certificates, diplomas, military discharge papers, driver's licenses, and immigration papers. For organizations, administrative records include certificates of incorporation and related documents. *Operational records* reflect tax and other certificates. *Intelligence records* are maintained by government agencies and represent security permissions and legal investigations. *Statistical records* can be obtained through an official questionnaire, as with the census, or from any of the other records that have been "cleansed" so as not to reflect personal information. Privacy safeguards are summarized in a far-reaching report by the Department of Health, Education, and Welfare (HEW 1973, pp. xx-xxi.):

1. There must be no personal data record-keeping systems whose very existence is secret.
2. There must be a way for an individual to find out what information about him is in a record and how it is used.
3. There must be a way for an individual to prevent information about him that was obtained for one purpose from being used or made available for other purposes without his consent.
4. There must be a way for an individual to correct or amend a record of identifiable information about him.
5. Any organization creating, maintaining, using, or disseminating records of identifiable personal data must assure the reliability of the data for their intended use and must take precautions to prevent misuse of the data.

The five principles are regarded as a Code of Fair Information Practice, emphasizing that privacy is a service that should be afforded to all citizens by other citizens, organizations, and the government in a free and open society.

PRIVACY ISSUES

The subject of privacy in all of its "multi-faceted dimensions" is of concern to many persons. Some individuals only wake up to the subject when their privacy is invaded and then quickly go back to sleep when the situation subsides, or they get tired of worrying about it. In the present context, cloud computing would seem to constitute a privacy threat to many persons and also organizations, because sensitive information is held by third-party service providers. However, having a third-party service provider is not a necessary condition for privacy invasion. The gang-of-three (government, employers, and education) would appear to be doing a good job with that. What are the specific issues about which we should be concerned? The topic has been addressed by the Privacy Rights Clearinghouse (PRC) in a document entitled "Privacy Today: A Review of Current Issues" developed by its director Dr. Beth Givens. (Givens 2009) The report lists twenty-three issues in privacy rights with a substantial description of each issue. The report highlights and summarizes the key issues and also contains links to special interest groups working on particular topics in that domain. We are going to concentrate on five subjects deemed relevant to the mission of this compendium:

o   Biometrics
o   Video surveillance and workplace monitoring
o   Data profiling
o   Behavioral tracking and targeting
o   Records on the Internet

A selection from the PRC list is also necessary because every privacy subject has its privacy point and twenty-three primary issues are more than we can usefully cover in this paper. Here is a simple straight-forward case of an individual personal privacy concern. "Joe Smith is a good runner and ran a local marathon in 3 hours and 20 minutes. The marathon organizer lists the name, age, finishing time, finisher's place, and home city and state of all finishers of the race on the Web. Joe has two concerns. He is a bit embarrassed, because a couple of years ago, he ran the same race in less than 3 hours. So, in this case Joe would prefer not to have the results published online for everyone to see – that is, if anyone besides runners would be interested.

Joe's friend Al has a different opinion. Al says, 'That is a great time Joe. My father, who is about your age, ran it in 3 hours and 10 minutes.' The second concern is more serious. Joe is 57 years old and is looking for a good position, since he was recently laid off. He is concerned that a prospective employer can Google him and determine his age from the online list of finishers, since age discrimination is a major concern for many employers in this country." If the race were run in Canada or Europe, on the other hand, the same information would not be available to outside persons, because of privacy laws.

We are going to present a descriptive technique that will apply the five selected dimensions, placing each dimension in a privacy-identity continuum.

Biometrics

The term *biometrics* refers to the use of a bodily characteristics for identification, which can be exact or probabilistic. If you have been in the ROTC, the military, law enforcement, possess a government security clearance, or have been born recently, you have an exact biometric identity consisting of your set of fingerprints on file in an official place. A person's DNA and retinal scan are also supposedly exact biometric identifiers. Clearly, an exact biometric marking does in fact identify a particular individual. However, the assignment of a name from an appropriate namespace is quite another thing. If the task is to link an individual with a specific name, then there is some probability involved. The picture on an official passport, driver's license, or government issued identification is also regarded as an exact identifier. But, how exact is exact? As mentioned before, there is some risk in linking name identification between two or more types of identity.

Less exact biometrics, such as facial recognition, has been employed in social situations to identify persons of interest – such as at sporting events. Using facial geometry and other visual clues, facial recognition technology has been very successful in criminal investigation. But, what about the identification and recording of persons in a lawful demonstration, guaranteed as a First Amendment right? Everyone knows there are at least two kind of demonstrators: those persons participating in the physical part of a demonstration because they genuinely believe in the cause, and those persons with nothing else to do on a Saturday afternoon. As Dr. Givens writes, "As a result, innocent people can be wrongly identified as criminal (false-positives), and known criminal and suspected terrorists can fail to be detected altogether (false-negatives).

Video Surveillance and Workplace Monitoring

Low-cost video surveillance systems are prevalent in modern society, and their use ranges from convenience stores to day-care centers. In fact, video surveillance is so pervasive that most people think nothing about being under the eye of the camera. In criminal investigation, video surveillance is a useful identifier, albeit within some probabilistic limits, and also as an investigative tool.

Collectively, video surveillance and workplace monitoring can provide information related to the following phenomena:

o   Facial recognition
o   Unproductive employment activity
o   Improper use of resources
o   Violation of conditions of service

Use of an employer's computer or other resources is a good case in point. Consider the following continuum:

Probably ——————————————————— **Not**
OK   **OK**

and the following activities:

o   Checking last night's baseball score
o   Finding the price of running shoes

o   Communicating with fellow workers
o   Communicating with non-work friends
o   Carrying on a romance within the same employer domain
o   Stealing company secrets

The placement of each activity in the continuum of workplace resources is easily achieved on a case-by-case basis. There are other forms of surveillance, such as Radio Frequency Identification (RFID) chips embedded in employee identification cards that can be used as an employee locator by recording when he or she leaves one room and enters another.

Keystroke monitors are sometimes used to determine ineffective use of equipment. Most employees do not seem to mind employee monitoring when on premises – but what can they do about it? Off premises and off hours surveillance and monitoring are quite another thing and exist as an open issue in privacy.

Data Profiling

Most of us are well represented in a multitude of gang-of-three databases, such as the tax bureau, social security administration, state motor vehicles office, education records, employment files, insurance, and health records. Information of this type can be regarded as the operational part of the fabric of life. We can temper the intrusion but not totally eliminate it, because it is paramount to identity determination and service management. Identities are linked by numbers, such as the social-security number, name, date of birth, telephone number, address and ZIP code, mother's maiden name, and even mother's birthday. It is even possible to find the social security number of an unrelated deceased person on the Web. Immigration records are also easily obtainable. The Privacy Act of 1974 and its amendments generally cover governmental data protection and profiling.

There is another form of data that is involuntarily collected about individuals where there is some choice involved, on the part of the individual, such as expenditures, lifestyle, Internet activity, political activity and donations, and so forth. Supermarket stores, bookstores, department stores, health stores, fitness centers, libraries, toll booths, big-ticket retailers, travel agencies, magazine publishers, and airlines – all contain personal data on individuals. An idea of interests, activities, and expenditures are available from credit card purchases, bank records, and operational files of business, governmental, and educational institutions. Thus, it is quite easy for an interested party to create a *data profile* of a person.

Pundits claim that profile data determines who or what we are. However, there is a tendency to interpret data based on the psychological perspective of the profiler. If you subscribe to "guns and ammo," does that indicate that you are a terrorist, member of the local shooting club, an Olympic athlete, worker in a sporting goods store that sells guns, or a medical professional who uses a service to provide magazines for the waiting room.

It has been reported that search providers turn over search queries of individuals to the agencies of the government. (Conti 2009, pp.259-298) This is a modern form of data profiling. A method, termed *chaffing,* is mentioned to widen the search domain and provide some protection. So, if you are going to search for a controversial person, you might also want to search for some non-threatening person to widen the search area.

Behavioral Tracking and Targeting

`Behavioral tracking and targeting is an area of privacy concern related to data profiling with emphasis on what a subject does. Here is a typical scenario. A subject rents a car and drives that vehicle out of state or out of the country by accident or by intention. When the car is turned in to the agency, the renter is charged an enormous penalty. The fine print in the contract was not read, because the renter is usually out of his or her element or just in a hurry. How did the agency know of the unfortunate travel? The car rental agency used a global positioning system (GPS) device to track the path of the vehicle. In addition to GPS tracking, license plate tracking, implemented through highway cameras, is also widely by state and local law enforcement officials. There is always a stated reason why organizations do things, but in the case of privacy, the main problem is the repurposing of collected data. Through data mining technology, computers can identify patterns based on happenstance, rather than purposeful activity. Here is another example: At the time this paragraph was written, the state of Arizona decided to take border control into its own hands. The federal government could do it and can do it, but we live in a large country with enough problems to go around. Getting the right person or an organization's attention at the right time usually takes some up front planning. Demonstrations ensue for varying reasons, including the possibility that certain outside people want to stir up trouble. Proper officials are looking into persons flying into Arizona with recently booked tickets for travel lasting only a few days and are doing some data mining to identify those persons. Are the identified persons demonstration instigators or a couple of grandparents attending a graduation ceremony. Regardless, they are prime candidates for behavioral tracking. In an era of supercomputing, piecing together a travel itinerary is not a major task. All that is needed is a subject to track.

The subject of behavioral tracking also includes the practice of collecting and compiling consumers' online activities, interests, preferences, and/or communications over time. (Givens 2009, 18 of 23) This form of behavioral targeting serves as the basis for advertising and other forms of marketing. Web browsing is a primary source of information in this regard.

There is also a growing trend by Internet service providers (ISPs) to use deep packet investigation (DPI) to look at email, Web sites visited, music, video sharing, and downloads by inspecting the data packets that constitute Internet traffic. This form of privacy intrusion is a major challenge to privacy advocates.

Records on the Internet

There is a tendency in society for persons in a political or geographical jurisdiction to be generally the same. This refers to attitudes, culture, psychological properties, and so forth. Between countries, however, there tend to be some differences between the two groups of people. People from Switzerland are different from people from England. The same idea holds true for people from Minnesota and Georgia, for example. We are referring to what is acceptable behavior, from a cultural viewpoint, or "would you like that person living next door."

The disclosure of public records in an open government is not sensitive to cultural differences, since the context for the information in government-managed files does not travel with the information. Citizens in one area may be more or less sensitive to the content of public information than persons from another – especially in a large country. The "one size fits all" mentality of public disclosure is a subject that frustrates privacy advocates.

Nevertheless, divorce records, criminal records, under-age convictions, bankruptcy proceedings, DIU convictions, motor vehicle records, and so forth, are all publically available through mailing list and information brokers. All an identity thief or stalker needs is a Social Security number and $19.95. The motivation for many, if not most, automobile breakins in modern times is an attempt to obtain personal information in the glove box, even thought the thief may also take a camera from the rear seat.

The appendix includes information on the Privacy Act of 1974, along with subsequent addendums to the law and relevant interpretations. The subject of privacy is a totally unstructured problem, and the privacy act has been a successful attempt at giving the problem some structure.

Privacy Analytics

Most individuals do not even know where they stand with regard to privacy. For example, a person might put their social history on Facebook, but bristle at the thought of identity theft and behavioral tracking. It would seem that a *privacy framework* would be useful for putting the various elements into proper perspective. We are going to propose a descriptive technique based on a radar diagram. Figure 1 gives a sample application based on the five privacy elements presented thus far.

The effective use of a PFD is open ended. In an appropriate context, it could represent privacy concerns with the values representing the "mass" committed to that element. In another context, it could represent the effort expended in a particular analytic situation. It could also represent the efficacy of various techniques applied to a specific case study.

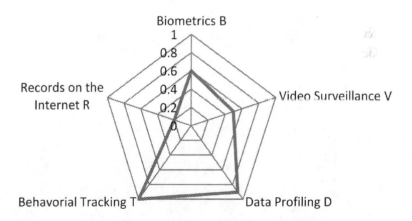

Figure 1. Privacy Framework Diagram (PFD).

REFERENCES

1   Conti, G. 2009. *Googling Security.* Upper Saddle River, NJ: Addison-Wesley.
2   Givens, B. 2009. Privacy Today: A Review of Current Issues. *Privacy Rights Clearinghouse. www.privacyrights.org/ar/Privacy-IssuesList.htm, (downloaded on 2/15/2010).*
3   Katzan, H. 1980. *Multinational Computer Systems: An Introduction of Transnational Data Flow and Data Regulation.* New York: Van Nostrand Reinhold Co.
4   Miller, A. 1971. *The Assault on Privacy: Computers, Data Banks, and Dossiers.* Ann Arbor: The University of Michigan Press.
5   U.S. Department of Health, Education, and Welfare (HEW) 1973. *Records, Computers, and the Rights of Citizens,* Cambridge: The M.I.T. Press.
6   Ware, W. 1977. Handling Personal Data, *Datamation* (October, 1977), pp. 83-87.
7   Westin, A.E. 1977. *Computers, Health Records, and Citizen's Rights,* Princeton: Petrocelli Books, Inc.
8   Westin, A.F. 1967. *Privacy and Freedom.* New York: Atheneum.

9

LIBERTY, FREEDOM, AND RIGHTS

INTRODUCTION

It is important to view privacy and identity in a larger context of liberty, freedom, and rights. Listen to Bertrand Russell. *Freedom in general may be defined as the absence of obstacles to the realization of desires.* (Russell 1940) While the definition avoids the issue of "freedom from" and "freedom to," it sets the stage for the limits to the authority of society over the individual. John Stuart Mill, the best known early American author on freedom, wisely pointed out in 1859:

> Though society is not founded on a contract, and though no good purpose is answered by inventing a contract in order to deduce social obligations from it, everyone who receives the protection of society owes a return for the benefit, and the fact of living in society renders it indispensable that each should be bound to observe a certain line of conduct towards the rest. This conduct consists, first in not injuring the interests of one another; or rather certain interests, which either by express legal provision or by tacit understanding, ought to be considered as rights; and secondly, in each person's bearing his

135

> share (to be fixed on some equitable principle) of
> the labours and sacrifices incurred for defending the
> society or its members from injury and molestation.
> These conditions society is justified in enforcing,
> at all costs to those who endearour to withhold
> fulfillment. (Mill 1859)

Mill's observations aptly set the stage for a brief discussion of individual liberty and effectively initiate an analysis of several key relevant topics ranging from the state, law, and morality to personal right and choice.

It would be inappropriate to imply from the quotation that individuals should not be concerned with affairs of other individuals – except in their own self-interest. Society is too dynamic and interdependent for that. On the other hand, an individual is most interested in his or her own well-being. One's self-interests are paramount, and the interference of society, except in extreme cases, is likely to be inappropriate.

Clearly, societal regulation is not fundamentally intended to restrain the actions of individuals, but rather, to help them. Government should provide benefits – either directly or indirectly – to individuals, instead of requiring that they acquire a corresponding service for themselves. The areas of health, education, trade, crime management, and transportation are obvious examples of societal concerns. While individuals are not accountable to society for their actions, traditional forms of social and legal punishment have resulted from certain actions that invade the domain of others.

The infringement by persons upon the interests of others does not alone justify the interference of society. In fact, Mill's principle of individual liberty promotes a single purpose:

> The principle is, that the sole end for which mankind
> are warranted, individually or collectively, in
> interfering with the liberty of action of any of their

number, is self-protection. That the only purpose for which power can be rightfully exercised over any member of a civilized community, against his will, is to prevent harm to others. (Mill *op cit.*)

Other popular objections to government interference are:

1. Actions are better performed by individuals than by government.
2. In cases where government performance excels over individual performance, actions are preferably performed by individuals for their own self-betterment.
3. Government interference into individual affairs adds unnecessarily to its power.

The preceding discussion represents the classic struggle between liberty and authority. The basic concepts, such as self-government, provide neither a solution to the problem of liberty vs. authority, nor a clear representation of the problem, if in fact, there is a problem. The notion of *tyranny-of-the-majority*, means that the individuals who exercise power are not always the same individuals over whom power is exercised.

FREEDOM

As a social concept, *freedom* refers to the relationship between individuals in an interpersonal environment. An individual is usually considered to be free when his or her condition exists without coercion or constraint imposed by another individual. Thus, a free individual can select goals and appropriate alternatives, and is not restricted in thought or action by the will or presence of another person. In a political sense, an individual is free when he or she is not restricted, as covered above, by the state or other authority.

The above notion of freedom can be enlarged somewhat by considering the conditions under which actions can be performed and the environment in which they are executed. The current thinking is that natural or societal conditions, defined in the broadest possible sense, constitute constraints on an individual's ability to establish goals and select among alternate courses of action; moreover, any knowledge that aids one in using existing conditions increases one's freedom. In addition, freedom is determined according to whether we have the power to achieve a goal or execute a selected course of action. Therefore, the absence of the means or power to do something is equivalent to the absence of freedom to do it. To sum up, freedom necessarily entails the following conditions:

1. The absence of coercion or restraint in any form by an individual, the state, or other authority that would prevent an individual from selecting and executing specific goals and taking certain courses of action
2. The absence of natural or societal conditions that would prevent the attainment of specific objectives
3. The possession of the power to, or the means of achieving, a specific objective

The conditions effectively equate *to be free* with *to be able to*. Clearly, the absence of the power and social means of achieving a selected goal is not necessarily restricted to simple cases where one person imposes restrictions on the activities of another.

The notion of *coercion* is relevant to the concept of freedom. In addition to physical forms of restraint, coercion also incorporates manipulation through the control of information required to make informed decisions. For example, an authoritarian society might manipulate and control the minds of individuals by governing the information and activities to which they are exposed. Through various forms of propaganda and conditioning, individuals can be made to favor the alternatives that their authority wants them to favor, by restricting knowledge of other alternatives. Persons, including legal entities, may not even be aware of the obstruction to freedom. Information extends the capacity for freedom of action, and a lack of information generally restricts that capacity. The lack of a possible alternate is not explicitly regarded as a lack of freedom but is regarded as a restraint of the freedom of choice.

The freedom from coercion or constraint by others is commonly known as *negative freedom*, which is most commonly associated with personal freedom. *Positive freedom*, on the other hand, is associated with the process of acting on one's own behalf, such as freedom from want, freedom of speech, or freedom in the choice of an employer. Powerful organization, through their control of resources, can limit the alternatives available to others, as in cases of economic monopoly. The existence of unequal power relates to unequal freedom of choice.

THE STATE, LAW, AND MORALITY

The essence of government can be regarded as the formalization of an underlying set of laws of behavior. The executive responsibility of government usually entails three classes of activity:

1. *Legislative activity:* establishing the desired rules of conduct.
2. *Judicial activity:* applying the rules of conduct to specific occurrences of appropriate events.
3. *Penal activity:* sanctioning those individuals who have disobeyed the rules of conduct.

A society is commonly regarded as a *state* if it contains a central agency for performing these three activities. Historically, the state performed two essential functions:

1. Maintenance of law and order
2. Defense against external enemies

Translated into modern ideas, the state's functions involve the welfare of individual citizens and the survival of the state as a sovereign entity.

A collection of people that interact, cooperate, and communicate is regarded as a *society*. A society will persist only if it has generally accepted rules of conduct. The rules need not be formalized in order for a society to survive. However, when formalized in the form of a government, rules are commonly known as *laws*. A collection of people with the same government is called a *country*.

Laws are a product of a sovereign state. (Such laws are regarded as *proper laws*, as compared to the *private regulations* of a family, club, or enterprise.) Most laws are historically or fundamentally based on *natural law*, a system of rights considered common to mankind. In modern times, natural law serves only as a standard of guidance when one is faced with conflicting ideologies. The term *natural* implies that a law is not legal, whereas *positive law* is conferred by the state and enforced through official sanction. Positive law is very precise, whereas natural law tends to be regarded as the broad moral consensus of the people. Many people believe that positive law is difficult or impossible to enforce if it runs contrary to natural law.

Although there may be no absolutely valid and unquestionable moral principles, some rights can be considered natural in the sense that they are proper and do not need to be guaranteed by law. These rights are possessed by all mankind and do not generally depend upon membership in a particular society. This class of rights is sometimes referred to as *human rights*.

OBLIGATION, LIBERTY, AND SOCIAL COST

The state, as a legal entity, has a right to the obedience of those for whom it performs services. However, the existence of a law that is contrary to natural law is sufficient reason for some individuals to disregard that law. On the other hand, many people give obedience to the state either out of habit or because it is reasonable to do so, without due regard to questions of morality and utilitarianism.

Looking at political obedience more closely, the question, Why should one show obedience to the state? is answered by one of three classes of theories: intrinsic, extrinsic, or organic. *Intrinsic theories* include such reasons as:

1. It has always been done *(traditionalism)*.
2. God has commanded us to do so *(divine right)*.
3. Authority is vested in the best people *(aristocracy)*.

Extrinsic theories cover such reasons as:

1. People have indirectly contracted to do so *(social contract)*,
2. It is necessary for the general welfare of society as a whole *(utilitarianism)*.

Intrinsic and extrinsic theories implicitly view the people and the state as fundamentally different entities; the citizens are distinct from and subordinate to the state. In an *organic theory*, the state represents the "better selves" of the people.

The notion of an absolute choice between obedience and resistance is perhaps not realistic, but it does reflect a concern for *liberty* or "for doing what one wants to do." The absence of interference (negative liberty) and the ability to do what one really wants to do (positive liberty) must be ultimately based on the *social cost* of maintaining obedience. Clearly, the cost of privacy regulation may represent an inordinately heavy economic burden that may ultimately offset any benefits derived from it.

RIGHT AND CHOICE

Hart claimed that, if there is any natural right at all, it is the equal right of people to be free. (Hart 1967) Berlin expounded on the subject:

> I wish to be a subject, not an object; to be moved by
> reason, by conscious purposes which are my own, not
> by causes which affect me, as it were, from outside. I
> wish to be somebody, not nobody; a doer – deciding,
> not being decided for, self-directed and not acted
> upon by external nature or by other men as if I were
> a thing, or an animal, or a slave incapable of playing
> a human role, that is, of conceiving goals and policies
> of my own and realizing them. (Berlin 1967)

The term *right* falls somewhere between law and morality.

There exists a segment of that which we loosely call *morality* that contains principles governing the degree to which one individual can determine how another individual can act. In this sense, the notion of right is associated with such familiar notions as justice, fairness, and obligation. Clearly, right, obligation, and duty are correlates. An individual, for example, has a right to personal autonomy. That right can be violated through a computer-based information system. An obligation to maintain personal autonomy is thereby incurred by the agency and beneficial user, and they have a duty to provide an appropriate level of data protection. *Even though a subject stands to benefit by the existence of such a system, the subject continues to possess the right to personal autonomy, and it is the duty of the agency and beneficial user to maintain that right.*

The existence of a one individual's right is related to another individual's freedom of choice. Through an irreversible promissory act, an individual *B* agrees to perform a particular task for individual *A*. *A* has a moral claim (i.e., a right) upon *B* to have *B* perform the task. However, *A* can waive the claim and release *B* from the obligation. Thus, *A* can act in such a way as to limit *B*'s freedom of choice. For example, an individual (*A*) waives his or her claim to personal autonomy, to some degree, when filling out an application for a credit card or a mortgage loan and thereby relieves the granting organization (*B*) of its social obligation. The logic of rights becomes apparent when a third party is involved – as in the case of subject, agency, and beneficial user. In this case, the beneficial user guarantees to the subject that a certain level of data protection will be maintained, and the agency guarantees the same degree of data protection to the beneficial user. Even though the subject is the person who will benefit from the data protection, he or she has limited control over the interactions between the other two parties.

It follows that rights are effectively owned by individuals, so that obligations refer to behavior of individuals and the behavior that can be expected of other individuals.

SUMMARY

Freedom is a social concept that refers to the relationship among individuals in an interpersonal environment. An individual who is free can select goals, appropriate alternatives, and is not restricted in thought or action by the will or presence of another person. Important considerations are conditions under which actions would be performed and the means by which they are performed. A key word in the concept of freedom is *coercion*. In general, freedom from coercion is embodied in two concepts: negative freedom and positive freedom.

The existence of a centralized agency for performing legislative, judicial, and penal activities in an organized society is commonly regarded as *state*. Laws are historically derived from natural law, which is a system of rights common to mankind. Legal laws are known as positive laws, which are conferred by the state and enforced through official sanction.

Rights are owned by individuals and refer to individual behavior (what a person can do) and the behavior that can be expected of others (what rights a person has). The existence of a right can be used to limit an individual's freedom of choice and has as its correlates obligation and duty.

REFERENCES

1 Berlin, I. 1967. Concepts of liberty. *Political Philosophy* (A. Quinton, editor), Oxford: Oxford University Press, p.149.

2 Bronowski, J. 1965. *Science and Human Values,* New York: Harper & Row.

3 Edwards, P. 1967. Freedom. *The Encyclopedia of Philosophy,* vol. 3, pp. 221-225, New York: The Free Press.

4 Hart, H. 1967. Are there any natural rights? *Political Philosophy* (A. Quinton, editor), Oxford: Oxford University Press, p.53.

5 Katzan, H. 1980. *Multinational Computer systems: An Introduction to Transnational Data Flow and Data Regulation,* New York: Van Nostrand Reinhold Co.

6 Mill, J. 1859. *On Liberty* (Published in R. Hutchins, editor, *Great Books of the Western World,* Volume 43, pp. 302-303. Chicago: Encyclopaedia Britannica, Inc. 1952.

7 Quinton, A. 1967. *Political Philosophy,* Oxford: Oxford University Press.

8 Russell, B. 1940. Freedom and Government. Ruth N. Anshen (ed.) *Freeedom: Its Meaning,* New York [secondary reference].

10

GLOBAL DATA
REGULATION

INTRODUCTION

Because of the ubiquitous use of computers and communications technology, there are no boundaries to the worldwide flow of data. The professional, scientific, and economic value of a modern world based on Internet technology is enormous. There are differing views, however, on the international flow of personal data that have resulted in various laws on data regulation. This paper gives a brief overview of this important topic.

To the layman, the widespread use of computer-based information systems must seem like a revolution, equivalent in scope and magnitude to the invention of movable type for book printing. The printed word has enabled the average person to become literate and thereby to actively participate in the dynamics of modern society. The rapid expansion of information technology and the widespread use of the Internet have made a lot of people uncomfortable on with the subject of computers and communications technology. To some individuals, computer people must seem to live in a world of their own.

To persons in the computer field, the task of staying abreast of a rapidly expanding technology has left little time and energy with which to be concerned with the social impact of the marriage of computer science and telecommunications technology. Early data processing systems were little more than mechanized version of manual procedures, so that many technologists became essentially unaware of the rapid expansion of and scope of on-line information systems.

In short, it is not a matter of knowing about and understanding recent advances in computers and telecommunications – technical people are very good at that – but rather that we are not exactly sure of what is being done with the new technology, and more importantly, where it will all lead. Perhaps, we need a generation of generalists to lead the way. They would enable us to enjoy the fruits of the information explosion and to take full advantage of the versatility of modern computers and the Internet.

REASONS FOR DATA REGULATION

Annoying dislocations invariable accompany emerging technology. One can easily imagine the plight of the blacksmith in the early 1900s, after the widespread acceptance of the automobile. However, a new type of dislocation is associated with information technology; it involves the erosion of personal privacy and the diminution of individual liberty. This is perhaps the most significant problem to be solved by our hypothetical generation of generalists, and the time to assess and fix the problem is in short supply.

The responsibility falls upon the shoulders of today's organizations to protect privacy and insure liberty as part of their normal recordkeeping activity. Many European countries have already passed laws governing the Transborder flow of information in order to protect the domain of their citizens. There are other reasons for regulating the flow of data and that may affect the manner in which multinational companies do business.

Essentially, we are talking about regulating technology, which in this case is the use of computers and Internet technology to manage data flow.

PRINCIPLES OF REGULATION

One way of looking at regulation is as the administration of society in the interest of its citizens. As a procedural technique, regulation is customarily regarded as being developed on either an *a* priori or an *a posteriori* basis. Development on an a priori basis involves a determination of rights and activities that should be protected and the subsequent enactment of regulations that should in fact protect those rights and activities. Adverse consequences are determined on a hypothetico-deductive basis, and laws are passed with the ultimate objective of preventing the undesirable consequences from occurring. Development on an a posteriori basis involves the identification of rights and activities that have been abused, from a regulatory point of view, and the subsequent enactment of laws that would forestall the widespread occurrence of those abuses. In short, adverse conditions are determined on an empirico-inductive basis, and the ultimate effect of those conditions is predicted. Laws are then passed to prevent the consequences from occurring.

The manner in which the desired results are obtained is significant. One approach involves the creation of a *controlling agency* to govern an activity that could result in undesirable consequences. Licenses are issued, and only those persons or organizations that have secured a license may engage in the activity – a driver's license for example, would fall into this category. Thus, the controlling agency achieves enforcement through the establishment of requirements for obtaining a license, by handling complaints and violations, and by performing investigatory work. The regulations and the controlling agency are commonly established by one act; this is known as the *omnibus approach*. The use of a controlling agency is normally associated with legislation determined on an a priori basis.

A second approach is to enact laws that make certain types of activities illegal and to establish, either explicitly or implicitly, corresponding penalties for infringement. This approach, which is essentially self-enforcing, requires a minimum level of government intervention and is enforced through the *judicial process*. Inherently flexible, this approach is normally associated with legislation determined on an a posteriori basis.

KEY FACTORS IN DATA REGULATION

One of the beneficial aspects of the present concern over data regulation is that it places the person about whom data are recorded in proper perspective. Whereas, such a person may be the object in an information system, he or she is regarded as the subject in data regulation. This usage of the word *subject* is intended to imply that a person should in fact have some control over the storage of relevant information.

More specifically, the *subject* is the person, natural or legal, about whom data are stored. The *beneficial user* is the organization or individual for whom processing is performed, and the *agency* is the computing system or organization that supplies the computer processing. In many cases, the beneficial user and the agency are associated with the same organization. In many cases, however, this will not be the case.

The beneficial user benefits from the data processing and has some control over the manner and time span in which the processing is performed. The agency need not be aware of how and when the processing is performed. The role of the subject, in this case, is self-evident.

The heart of the matter is *data protection,* which normally refers to the protection of rights of individuals. While the concept may also apply to groups of individuals, such as organizations or nations, the individual aspect of the issue raises question of privacy and liberty. Clearly, *privacy,* in this instance, refers to the claim if persons to determine when, how, and to what extent information about them is disclosed. It is important to recognize that privacy inherently incorporates freedom from intrusion and freedom of thought, choice, and action. Thus, the notion of privacy notably extends beyond the realm of information resources.

CONSIDERATIONS IN DATA REGULATION

One of the primary objectives in regulating data flow is to protect against the negative consequences of modern information technology. Thus, data regulation can be viewed as the balancing of the freedom and rights of the individual with common interest of society. This process, normally interpreted as the stabilizing of information technology through the use of legal procedures, has in itself negative consequences; that is, laws and tariffs may seriously disrupt the flow of information upon which modern society is dependent. In fact, many people feel that the free international flow of information is a fundamental aspect of a comprehensive human rights program.

Some countries resist the free flow of information across their borders because that information may erode their authority and control over their citizens. Others are concerned about the erosion of culture and traditional values. Still others are concerned about an increasing dependence on foreign information systems. Lastly, some countries for various reasons simply have something to hide.

PRACICAL ISSUES IN DATA REGULATION

Although computers and modern information systems, including the Internet, have not created the human rights issue, it is important to recognize that one of the basic methods of sustaining human rights is nevertheless achieved through the free flow of information. However, considerations of human rights, freedom of expression, and the invasion of privacy must be kept separate from the technical factors involved. Information technology can only provide a means of protecting privacy and promoting the unrestricted flow of information across international boundaries.

The substance of privacy laws effectively determines that the technical means of achieving privacy in information systems be commensurate with the level of risk involved. Thus, the level of security provided by an information system can be expected to depend upon the sensitivity of the data. Clearly, the cost of obtaining restricted data through the penetration of information systems would not, in general, exceed the value of the information. An important final consideration is that even though the data may not be sensitive, the manner in which it is used may constitute an invasion of privacy.

Practically speaking, a clear definition of what constitutes private and personal information is lacking. As a substitute for a sensitivity order of personal data, there is a general belief that more sensitive data are positively correlated with the degree of seriousness of an invasion of privacy and the need for data protection. For example, relatively unimportant data such as family status and hobbies usually have low sensitivity, while credit and other financial data have high sensitivity. It would seem that two controls are needed:

1. Measures must exist to protect against unauthorized new use of data.
2. Data protection must exist independently of the agency and its locations.

The most important aspect of controls over the use of data is whether they are enforceable, and why it is necessary in general principles.

DATA VAULTS, DATA HAVENS, AND RELATED CONCEPTS

There is a growing concern over the misuse of information by businesses and government. Data vaults and data havens are concepts employed to prevent the misuse or even the use of information.

A *data vault* is an operational situation wherein data from one country are stored and processed in another country in order to obtain special protection for the parties involved. A company may assure its clients that personal information is stored in a foreign country beyond

THE LITTLE BOOK OF CLOUD COMPUTING

the reach of authorities. A form of storage of this type constitutes a data vault when data-protection laws guard against disclosure.

A *data haven* is an operational situation wherein data from one country are stored and processed in another country because the latter's data protection laws are lenient and permit disclosure that would be illegal in the originating country.

Both data vaults and data havens are the reasons that data protection laws have been passed by several countries. It is difficult, however, to enforce data protection laws when facilities cannot be physically inspected. In the modern Internet environment, it may not be possible to determine where the agency actually stores data, such that the subject and the beneficial user have no knowledge of the physical storage location.

THE ECONOMICS AND POLITICS
OF DATA REGULATION

Although the preservation of individual freedom may be an important motivating factor behind data protection legislation, it is by no means the only factor, and it may not even be the primary factor. In fact, many people feel that the main reasons for data regulation may be economic and political. This section gives a brief overview of economic and political issues.

It can be equitably stated that the actors in the data regulation scenario are divided into two camps: those who favor regulation and those who do not. The parties favoring regulation state that they do so for economic, political, or libertarian reasons. The parties who oppose regulation also give economic, political, or libertarian justification for their viewpoint, but their emphasis is primarily economic. Some of the reasons for favoring the regulation of Transborder data flow are:

1. Use of foreign (computer) service bureaus and computer facilities constitutes an economic drain on a country.

Introducing restriction on transborder data transfer is an effective means of protecting national services against foreign competition.

2. Regulation of transborder data transfer can be used as a means of establishing a national computer industry, by restricting the hardware, software, and services that can be developed or marketed in a country.

3. Transborder data regulation can be used as a means of imposing taxes and other sanctions on transborder data traffic.

4. Transborder data regulation can be used to reduce the level of dependence of country on another and permit a country to retain control over its infrastructure.

5. A general fear exists that governments will invade individual privacy unless there is some form of data protection.

In addition, there is also a general belief that unrestricted transborder data flow will create a technological dependence on countries that lead in communications and Internet technology.

Reasons that have been observed for opposing transborder data flow are:

1. Different countries may adopt different data protection laws, thereby increasing the cost of compliance and obstructing the timely flow of information.

2. Data protection laws may result in restraint of foreign competition, resulting in higher costs to users and a possible deterioration of service.

3. Restricting the free flow of information will hamper the economic growth of countries, since no nation is completely self-sufficient with regard to information technology.

4. Restrictive transborder data flow regulations can disrupt the internal operation of many multinational companies.

5. Certain types of data regulation will result in non-optimal solutions to computer processing problems.

6. Nations in the global society are technically and economically interdependent, and many services, such as reservations, production scheduling, and shipping inherently require the transborder flow of data.

In this domain, there is an underlying attitude that communications and Internet technology are national resources that must be balance with existing natural resources.

QUICK SUMMARY

1. The benefits of modern information technology must be weighed against the social, economic, and political concerns that are generated as the byproducts of advanced technology.
2. One means of controlling the impact of information technology is to regulate it.
3. Three parties are involved with data regulation: the subject, the beneficial user, and the agency.
4. The heart of the issue is personal privacy and data protection.

REFERENCES

1   Benjamin, A. 1979. Privacy, security, and responsibility. *Transnational Data Regulation: The Realities*, Uxbridge: Online Conferences, Ltd.
2   Bing, J. 1979. Transborder data flows: Some legal issues and possible effects on business practices. *Transnational Data Regulation: The Realities*, Uxbridge: Online Conferences, Ltd.
3   Edwards, P. 1967. Freedom. *The Encyclopedia of Philosophy*, vol. 3, pp. 221-225, New York: The Free Press.
4   Hart, H. 1967. Are there any natural rights? *Political Philosophy* (A. Quinton, editor), Oxford: Oxford University Press, p.53.
5   Katzan, H. 1980. *Multinational Computer systems: An Introduction to Transnational Data Flow and Data Regulation*, New York: Van Nostrand Reinhold Co.
6   Miller, A. 1971. *The Assault on Privacy: Computers, Data Banks, and Dossiers*. Ann Arbor: The University of Michigan Press.

ADDENDUM: COMBINED REFERENCES

ACLU of Northern California. 2010. *Cloud Computing: Storm Warning for Privacy?* www.dotrights.org, (downloaded 3/11/2010).

Anderson, C. 2006. *The Long Tail*. New York: Hyperion.

Bacon, Sir Francis. 1605. *Advancement of Learning*. (Republished in the *Great Books of the Western World*. Volume 30, Robert Maynard Hutchins, Editor in Chief, Chicago: Encyclopedia Britannica, Inc., 1952).

Benjamin, A. 1979. Privacy, security, and responsibility. *Transnational Data Regulation: The Realities*, Uxbridge: Online Conferences, Ltd.

Berlin, I. 1967. Concepts of liberty. *Political Philosophy* (A. Quinton, editor), Oxford: Oxford University Press, p.149.

Bing, J. 1979. Transborder data flows: Some legal issues and possible effects on business practices. *Transnational Data Regulation: The Realities*, Uxbridge: Online Conferences, Ltd.

Black, M. 1952. Identity of Indiscernibles. *Mind* 61:153. (Secondary reference.)

Bronowski, J. 1965. *Science and Human Values,* New York: Harper & Row.

Brunette, G. and R. Mogull (ed). 2009. *Security Guidance for Critical Areas of Focus in Cloud Computing V2.1.* Cloud Security Alliance, December 2009.

Campbell, J. 1989. *The Improbable Machine,* New York: Simon & Schuster, Inc.

Carraro, G. 2007. Cost per feature vs. cost per tenant. *Microsoft Corporation,* blogs.msdn.com/gianpaolo/archive.

Carraro, G. 2008. I don't believe we are still talking about whether SaaS = multi-tenancy ... . *Microsoft Corporation,* blogs.msdn.com/gianpaolo/archive.

Carraro, G. 2008. Monetization: the next frontier of SaaS/S+S architecture. *Microsoft Corporation,* blogs.msdn.com/gianpaolo/archive.

Cavoukian, A. 2009. *Privacy in the Clouds.* Toronto: Information and Privacy Commission of Ontario (www.ipc.on.ca).

Cavoukian, A. 2010. 7 Laws of Identity: The Case for Privacy-Embedded Laws of Identity I the Digital Age." Toronto: Information and Privacy Commission of Ontario (www.ipc.on.ca).

Center for Digital Democracy (CDD). 2009. *Online Behavioral Tracking and Targeting: Legislative Primer September 2009.* www.democraticmedia.org/privacy-legislative-primer. (downloaded 3/11/2010).

Chappell, D. 2008. Introducing the Azure Services Platform. *Microsoft Corporation.*

Chappell, D. 2009. Introducing the Windows Azure Platform. *Microsoft Corporation.*

Charney, S. 2008. Establishing End to End Trust. *Microsoft Corporation.*

Chong, F. 2008. Application Marketplaces and the Money Trail. *Microsoft Corporation.*

Chong, F. and G. Carraro. 2006. Architecture Strategies for Catching the Long Tail. *Microsoft Corporation.*

Cloud Computing: The Evolution of Software-as-a-Science. *Arizona State University W.P. Carey School of Business,* June 4, 2008, knowledge. wpcarey.asu.edu, (2008).

Conti, G. 2009. *Googling Security.* Upper Saddle River, NJ: Addison-Wesley.

Dempster, A. 1967, "Upper and Lower Probabilities Induced by a Multivalued Mapping," *The Annals of Statistics* 28:325-339.

Edwards, P. 1967. Freedom. *The Encyclopedia of Philosophy,* vol. 3, pp. 221-225, New York: The Free Press.

Federal Bureau of Investigation. 2004. *Privacy Impact Assessment.* www.fbi.gov/biometrics.htm. (downloaded 2/20/2010).

Ferrario, R. and N. Guardino. 2008. Towards an Ontological Foundation for Services Science. *Proceedings of the Future Internet Symposium,* Vienna Austria, 28-30 September 2008.

Foley, M. 2008. *Microsoft 2.0,* Indianapolis: Wiley Publishing, Inc.

Gellman, R. 2009. *Privacy in the Clouds: Risks to Privacy and Confidentiality form Cloud Computing.* World Privacy Forum (February 23, 2009).

Givens, B. 2009. Privacy Today: A Review of Current Issues. *Privacy Rights Clearinghouse. www.privacyrights.org/ar/Privacy-IssuesList.htm, (downloaded on 2/15/2010).*

Gruber, T. 2008. Ontology. *Encyclopedia of Database Systems*, Liu, L. and M. Ozsu (Eds.), Springer-Verlag,

Hart, H. 1967. Are there any natural rights? *Political Philosophy* (A. Quinton, editor), Oxford: Oxford University Press, p.53.

IBM Corporation. 2009. The Benefits of Cloud Computing. Form DW03004-USEN-00.

Kant, I. 1787. *Critique of Pure Reason.* (Republished in *Basic Writings of Kant.* Allen W. Wood, Editor, New York: The Modern Library, 2001).

Katzan, H. 1975. *Computer Data Management and Data Base Technology*, New York: Van Nostrand Reinhold Co.

Katzan, H. 1980. *Multinational Computer Systems: An Introduction to Transnational Data Flow and Data Regulation.* New York: Van Nostrand Reinhold Co.

Katzan, H. 1986. *Operating Systems: A Pragmatic Approach (2e).* Hoboken, NJ: John Wiley and Sons.

Katzan, H. 1992. *Managing Uncertainty: A Pragmatic Approach*, New York: Van Nostrand Reinhold Co.

Katzan, H. 2008. Categorical Analytics Based on Consensus Theory. *Journal of Business and Economics Research*, 6(8), 89-102.

Katzan, H. 2008. Cloud Computing, I-Service, and IT Service Provisioning. *Journal of Service Science*, 1(2):57-64.

Katzan, H. 2008. *Service Science: Concepts, Technology, Management*, New York: iUniverse, Inc.

Katzan, H. 2009. Cloud Computing Economics: Democratization and Monetization of Services. *Journal of Business & Economics Research*, 7(6):1-11.

Katzan, H. 2009. Cloud Software Service: Concepts, Technology, Economics. *Service Science*, 1(4):256-269.

Knorr, E and G. Gruman. 2008. What cloud computing really means. *InfoWorld*, April 07, 2008, www.infoworld.com.

Martin, R and J. Hoover. 2008. Guide to Cloud Computing. *Information Week*, June 21, 2008, www.informationweek.com.

Mell, P. and T. Grance. 2009a. The NIST Definition of Cloud Computing. National Institute of Standards and Technology, Information Technology Laboratory, Version 15, 10-7-09. (http://www.csrc.nist.gov/groups/SNS/cloud-comjputing/index.html)

Mell, P., Badger, L., and T. Grance. 2009b. Effectively and Securely Using the Cloud Computing Paradigm. National Institute of Standards and Technology, Information Technology Laboratory, 10-7-09. (http://www.csrc.nist.gov/groups/SNS/cloud-comjputing/index.html)

Mill, J. 1859. *On Liberty* (Published in R. Hutchins, editor, *Great Books of the Western World*, Volume 43, pp. 302-303. Chicago: Encyclopaedia Britannica, Inc. 1952.

Miller, A. 1971. *The Assault on Privacy: Computers, Data Banks, and Dossiers*. Ann Arbor: The University of Michigan Press.

Miller, M. 2008. Cloud Computing: Web-Based Applications That Change the Way You Work and Collaborate Online, Indianapolis: Que Publishing.

Mundie, C., de Vries, P., Haynes, P., and M. Corwine. 2002. Trustworthy Computing. *Microsoft Corporation.*

Neapolitan, R. 1990. *Probabilistic Reasoning in Expert Systems: Theory and Applications,* New York: John Wiley & Sons, Inc.

Nelson, M. 2009. Cloud Computing and Public Policy. *Briefing Paper for the ICCP Technology Foresight Forum.* JT03270509, DATI/ICP(2009)17.

OECD 2010. OECD Guidelines on the Protection of Privacy and Transborder Flows of Personal Data. www.oecd.org. (downloaded 3/23/2010).

Perry, G. 2008., How Cloud & Utility Computing are Different. *GigaSpace Technologies,* February 28, 2008, www.gigacom.com.

Quinton, A. 1967. *Political Philosophy,* Oxford: Oxford University Press.

Rappa, M. 2004. The utility business model and the future of computing services. *IBM Systems Journal,* 43(1):32-41.

Reese, G. 2009. *Cloud Application Architectures: Building Applications and Infrastructure in the Cloud,* Sebastopol, CA: O'Reilly Media, Inc.

Russell, B. 1912. *The Problems of Philosophy.* (Republished by Barnes & Noble, New York, 2004).

Russell, B. 1919. *Introduction to Mathematical Philosophy.* (Republished by Barnes & Noble, New York, 2005).

Russell, B. 1940. Freedom and Government. Ruth N. Anshen (ed.) *Freeedom: Its Meaning,* New York [secondary reference].

Salido, J. and P. Voon. 2010. A Guide to Data Governance for Privacy, Confidentiality, and Compliance: Part 1. The Case for Data Governance. Microsoft Corporation,

Shafer, G. 1976, *A Mathematical Theory of Evidence*, Princeton, NJ: Princeton University Press.

Shinder, D. 2009. Microsoft Azure: Security in the Cloud. WindowSecurity.com (downloaded 1/27/2010).

Smith, Adam. 1776. *The Wealth of Nations*, published as "An Inquiry Into the Nature and Causes of the Wealth of Nations" in London, England.

Sowa, J. 2000. *Knowledge Representation: Logical, Philosophical and Computational Foundations*, Brooks Cole Publishing.

Stroll, A. 1967. *Identity*. (Entry in *The Encyclopedia of Philosophy*, Volume 4, Paul Edwards, Editor in Chief, New York: Macmillan Publishing Co., 1967).

U.S. Department of Health, Education, and Welfare (HEW) 1973. *Records, Computers, and the Rights of Citizens*, Cambridge: The M.I.T. Press.

Utility Based Cloud Power. *Computers Journal*, February 12, 2009, www.dirjournal.com, (2009).

Ware, W. 1977. Handling Personal Data, *Datamation* (October, 1977), pp. 83-87.

Web Hosting Fan. 2009. The Security and Privacy Concerns of Cloud Computing. September 24, 2009. www.webhostingfan.com/page/13 (downloaded 3/2/2010).

Westin, A.E. 1977. *Computers, Health Records, and Citizen's Rights,* Princeton: Petrocelli Books, Inc.

Westin, A.F. 1967. *Privacy and Freedom.* New York: Atheneum.

Wikipedia. 2008. Software as a Service. www.wikipedia.com.

Wikipedia. 2010. *Cloud Computing.* http://en.wikipedia.org/wiki/ Cloud_computing. (Downloaded 01/29/2010).

Youseff, L., Butrico, M., and D. Da Silva. 2009. *Toward a Unified Ontology of Cloud Computing.* (Available from the following: (lyouseff@cs.uscb.edu), (butrico@us.ibm.com), and (dilmasilva@ us.ibm.com).

APPENDIX: PRIVACY ACT OF 1974

The Privacy Act of 1974
(5 U.S.C. § 552a)

§ 552a. Records maintained on individuals

(a) Definitions.

For purposes of this section--

> (1) the term "agency" means agency as defined in section 552(e) of this title;

> (2) the term "individual" means a citizen of the United States or an alien lawfully admitted for permanent residence;

> (3) the term "maintain" includes maintain, collect, use, or disseminate;

> (4) the term "record" means any item, collection, or grouping of information about an individual that is maintained by an agency, including, but not limited to, his education, financial transactions, medical history, and criminal or employment history and that contains his name, or the identifying number, symbol, or other identifying particular assigned to the individual, such as a finger or voice print or a photograph;

> (5) the term "system of records" means a group of any records under the control of any agency from which information is retrieved by the name of the individual or by some identifying number, symbol, or other identifying particular assigned to the individual;

(6) the term "statistical record" means a record in a system of records maintained for statistical research or reporting purposes only and not used in whole or in part in making any determination about an identifiable individual, except as provided by section 8 of title 13;

(7) the term "routine use" means, with respect to the disclosure of a record, the use of such record for a purpose which is compatible with the purpose for which it was collected;

(8) the term "matching program"--

(A) means any computerized comparison of--

(i) two or more automated systems of records or a system of records with non-Federal records for the purpose of--

(I) establishing or verifying the eligibility of, or continuing compliance with statutory and regulatory requirements by, applicants for, recipients or beneficiaries of, participants in, or providers of services with respect to, cash or in-kind assistance or payments under Federal benefit programs, or

(II) recouping payments or delinquent debts under such Federal benefit programs, or

(ii) two or more automated Federal personnel or payroll systems of records or a system of Federal personnel or payroll records with non-Federal records,

(B) but does not include--

(i) matches performed to produce aggregate statistical data without any personal identifiers;

(ii) matches performed to support any research or statistical project, the specific data of which may not be used to make decisions concerning the rights, benefits, or privileges of specific individuals;

(iii) matches performed, by an agency (or component thereof) which performs as its principal function any activity pertaining to the enforcement of criminal laws, subsequent to the initiation of a specific criminal or civil law enforcement investigation of a named person or persons for the purpose of gathering evidence against such person or persons;

(iv) matches of tax information (I) pursuant to section 6103(d) of the Internal Revenue Code of 1986, (II) for purposes of tax administration as defined in section 6103(b)(4) of such Code, (III) for the purpose of intercepting a tax refund due an individual under authority granted by section 404(e), 464, or 1137 of the Social Security Act; or (IV) for the purpose of intercepting a tax refund due an individual under any other tax refund intercept program authorized by statute which has been determined by the Director of the Office of Management and Budget to contain verification, notice, and hearing requirements that are substantially similar to the procedures in section 1137 of the Social Security Act;

(v) matches--

(I) using records predominantly relating to Federal personnel, that are performed for routine administrative purposes (subject to guidance provided by the Director of the Office of Management and Budget pursuant to subsection (v)); or

(II) conducted by an agency using only records from systems of records maintained by that agency; if the purpose of the match is not to take any adverse financial, personnel, disciplinary, or other adverse action against Federal personnel

(vi) matches performed for foreign counterintelligence purposes or to produce background checks for security clearances of Federal personnel or Federal contractor personnel;

(vii) matches performed incident to a levy described in section 6103(k)(8) of the Internal Revenue Code of 1986; or

(viii) matches performed pursuant to section 202(x)(3) or 1611(e)(1) of the Social Security Act (42 U.S.C. 402(x)(3), 1382(e)(1));

(9) the term "recipient agency" means any agency, or contractor thereof, receiving records contained in a system of records from a source agency for use in a matching program;

(10) the term "non-Federal agency" means any State or local government, or agency thereof, which receives records

contained in a system of records from a source agency for use in a matching program;

(11) the term "source agency" means any agency which discloses records contained in a system of records to be used in a matching program, or any State or local government, or agency thereof, which discloses records to be used in a matching program;

(12) the term "Federal benefit program" means any program administered or funded by the Federal Government, or by any agent or State on behalf of the Federal Government, providing cash or in-kind assistance in the form of payments, grants, loans, or loan guarantees to individuals; and

(13) the term "Federal personnel" means officers and employees of the Government of the United States, members of the uniformed services (including members of the Reserve Components), individuals entitled to receive immediate or deferred retirement benefits under any retirement program of the Government of the United States (including survivor benefits).

(h) Conditions of disclosure.

No agency shall disclose any record which is contained in a system of records by any means of communication to any person, or to another agency, except pursuant to a written request by, or with the prior written consent of, the individual to whom the record pertains, unless disclosure of the record would be--

(1) to those officers and employees of the agency which maintains the record who have a need for the record in the performance of their duties;

(2) required under section 552 of this title;

(3) for a routine use as defined in subsection (a)(7) of this section and described under subsection (e)(4)(D) of this section;

(4) to the Bureau of the Census for purposes of planning or carrying out a census or survey or related activity pursuant to the provisions of title 13;

(5) to a recipient who has provided the agency with advance adequate written assurance that the record will be used solely as a statistical research or reporting record, and the record is to be transferred in a form that is not individually identifiable;

(6) to the National Archives and Records Administration as a record which has sufficient historical or other value to warrant its continued preservation by the United States Government, or for evaluation by the Archivist of the United States or the designee of the Archivist to determine whether the record has such value;

(7) to another agency or to an instrumentality of any governmental jurisdiction within or under the control of the United States for a civil or criminal law enforcement activity if the activity is authorized by law, and if the head of the agency or instrumentality has made a written request to the agency which maintains the record specifying the particular portion desired and the law enforcement activity for which the record is sought;

(8) to a person pursuant to a showing of compelling circumstances affecting the health or safety of an individual if upon such disclosure notification is transmitted to the last known address of such individual;

(9) to either House of Congress, or, to the extent of matter within its jurisdiction, any committee or subcommittee thereof, any joint committee of Congress or subcommittee of any such joint committee;

(10) to the Comptroller General, or any of his authorized representatives, in the course of the performance of the duties of the Government Accountability Office;

(11) pursuant to the order of a court of competent jurisdiction; or

(12) to a consumer reporting agency in accordance with section 3711(e) of title 31.

(c) Accounting of certain disclosures.

Each agency, with respect to each system of records under its control, shall--

(1) except for disclosures made under subsections (b)(1) or (b)(2) of this section, keep an accurate accounting of--

(A) the date, nature, and purpose of each disclosure of a record to any person or to another agency made under subsection (b) of this section; and

(B) the name and address of the person or agency to whom the disclosure is made;

(2) retain the accounting made under paragraph (1) of this subsection for at least five years or the life of the record, whichever is longer, after the disclosure for which the accounting is made;

(3) except for disclosures made under subsection (b)(7) of this section, make the accounting made under paragraph (1) of this subsection available to the individual named in the record at his request; and

(4) inform any person or other agency about any correction or notation of dispute made by the agency in accordance with subsection (d) of this section of any record that has been disclosed to the person or agency if an accounting of the disclosure was made.

(d) Access to records.

Each agency that maintains a system of records shall--

(1) upon request by any individual to gain access to his record or to any information pertaining to him which is contained in the system, permit him and upon his request, a person of his own choosing to accompany him, to review the record and have a copy made of all or any portion thereof in a form comprehensible to him, except that the agency may require the individual to furnish a written statement authorizing discussion of that individual's record in the accompanying person's presence;

(2) permit the individual to request amendment of a record pertaining to him and--

(A) not later than 10 days (excluding Saturdays, Sundays, and legal public holidays) after the date of receipt of such request, acknowledge in writing such receipt; and

(B) promptly, either--

(i) make any correction of any portion thereof which the individual believes is not accurate, relevant, timely, or complete; or

(ii) inform the individual of its refusal to amend the record in accordance with his request, the reason for the refusal, the procedures established by the agency for the individual to request a review of that refusal by the head of the agency or an officer designated by the head of the agency, and the name and business address of that official;

(3) permit the individual who disagrees with the refusal of the agency to amend his record to request a review of such refusal, and not later than 30 days (excluding Saturdays, Sundays, and legal public holidays) from the date on which the individual requests such review, complete such review and make a final determination unless, for good cause shown, the head of the agency extends such 30-day period; and if, after his review, the reviewing official also refuses to amend the record in accordance with the request, permit the individual to file with the agency a concise statement setting forth the reasons for his disagreement with the refusal of the agency, and notify the individual of the provisions for judicial review of the reviewing official's determination under subsection (g)(1)(A) of this section;

(4) in any disclosure, containing information about which the individual has filed a statement of disagreement, occurring after the filing of the statement under paragraph (3) of this subsection, clearly note any portion of the record which is disputed and provide copies of the statement and, if the agency deems it appropriate, copies of a concise statement of the reasons of the agency for not making the amendments requested, to persons or other agencies to whom the disputed record has been disclosed; and

(5) nothing in this section shall allow an individual access to any information compiled in reasonable anticipation of a civil action or proceeding.

(e) Agency requirements.

Each agency that maintains a system of records shall--

(1) maintain in its records only such information about an individual as is relevant and necessary to accomplish a purpose of the agency required to be accomplished by statute or by executive order of the President;

(2) collect information to the greatest extent practicable directly from the subject individual when the information may result in adverse determinations about an individual's rights, benefits, and privileges under Federal programs;

(3) inform each individual whom it asks to supply information, on the form which it uses to collect the information or on a separate form that can be retained by the individual--

(A) the authority (whether granted by statute, or by executive order of the President) which authorizes the solicitation of the information and whether disclosure of such information is mandatory or voluntary;

(B) the principal purpose or purposes for which the information is intended to be used;

(C) the routine uses which may be made of the information, as published pursuant to paragraph (4)(D) of this subsection; and

(D) the effects on him, if any, of not providing all or any part of the requested information;

(4) subject to the provisions of paragraph (11) of this subsection, publish in the Federal Register upon establishment

or revision a notice of the existence and character of the system of records, which notice shall include--

(A) the name and location of the system;

(B) the categories of individuals on whom records are maintained in the system;

(C) the categories of records maintained in the system;

(D) each routine use of the records contained in the system, including the categories of users and the purpose of such use;

(E) the policies and practices of the agency regarding storage, retrievability, access controls, retention, and disposal of the records;

(F) the title and business address of the agency official who is responsible for the system of records;

(G) the agency procedures whereby an individual can be notified at his request if the system of records contains a record pertaining to him;

(H) the agency procedures whereby an individual can be notified at his request how he can gain access to any record pertaining to him contained in the system of records, and how he can contest its content; and

(I) the categories of sources of records in the system;

(5) maintain all records which are used by the agency in making any determination about any individual with such accuracy, relevance, timeliness, and completeness as is

reasonably necessary to assure fairness to the individual in the determination;

(6) prior to disseminating any record about an individual to any person other than an agency, unless the dissemination is made pursuant to subsection (b)(2) of this section, make reasonable efforts to assure that such records are accurate, complete, timely, and relevant for agency purposes;

(7) maintain no record describing how any individual exercises rights guaranteed by the First Amendment unless expressly authorized by statute or by the individual about whom the record is maintained or unless pertinent to and within the scope of an authorized law enforcement activity;

(8) make reasonable efforts to serve notice on an individual when any record on such individual is made available to any person under compulsory legal process when such process becomes a matter of public record;

(9) establish rules of conduct for persons involved in the design, development, operation, or maintenance of any system of records, or in maintaining any record, and instruct each such person with respect to such rules and the requirements of this section, including any other rules and procedures adopted pursuant to this section and the penalties for noncompliance;

(10) establish appropriate administrative, technical, and physical safeguards to insure the security and confidentiality of records and to protect against any anticipated threats or hazards to their security or integrity which could result in substantial harm, embarrassment, inconvenience, or unfairness to any individual on whom information is maintained;

(11) at least 30 days prior to publication of information under paragraph (4)(D) of this subsection, publish in the Federal Register notice of any new use or intended use of the information in the system, and provide an opportunity for interested persons to submit written data, views, or arguments to the agency; and

(12) if such agency is a recipient agency or a source agency in a matching program with a non-Federal agency, with respect to any establishment or revision of a matching program, at least 30 days prior to conducting such program, publish in the Federal Register notice of such establishment or revision.

(f) Agency rules.

In order to carry out the provisions of this section, each agency that maintains a system of records shall promulgate rules, in accordance with the requirements (including general notice) of section 553 of this title, which shall--

(1) establish procedures whereby an individual can be notified in response to his request if any system of records named by the individual contains a record pertaining to him;

(2) define reasonable times, places, and requirements for identifying an individual who requests his record or information pertaining to him before the agency shall make the record or information available to the individual;

(3) establish procedures for the disclosure to an individual upon his request of his record or information pertaining to him, including special procedure, if deemed necessary, for the disclosure to an individual of medical records, including psychological records, pertaining to him;

(4) establish procedures for reviewing a request from an individual concerning the amendment of any record or information pertaining to the individual, for making a determination on the request, for an appeal within the agency of an initial adverse agency determination, and for whatever additional means may be necessary for each individual to be able to exercise fully his rights under this section; and

(5) establish fees to be charged, if any, to any individual for making copies of his record, excluding the cost of any search for and review of the record.

The Office of the Federal Register shall biennially compile and publish the rules promulgated under this subsection and agency notices published under subsection (e)(4) of this section in a form available to the public at low cost.

(g)(1) Civil remedies.

Whenever any agency--

(A) makes a determination under subsection (d)(3) of this section not to amend an individual's record in accordance with his request, or fails to make such review in conformity with that subsection;

(B) refuses to comply with an individual request under subsection (d)(1) of this section;

(C) fails to maintain any record concerning any individual with such accuracy, relevance, timeliness, and completeness as is necessary to assure fairness in any determination relating to the qualifications, character, rights, or opportunities of, or benefits to the individual that may be made on the basis of such record, and consequently a determination is made which is adverse to the individual; or

(D) fails to comply with any other provision of this section, or any rule promulgated thereunder, in such a way as to have an adverse effect on an individual, the individual may bring a civil action against the agency, and the district courts of the United States shall have jurisdiction in the matters under the provisions of this subsection.

(2)(A) In any suit brought under the provisions of subsection (g)(1)(A) of this section, the court may order the agency to amend the individual's record in accordance with his request or in such other way as the court may direct. In such a case the court shall determine the matter de novo.

(B) The court may assess against the United States reasonable attorney fees and other litigation costs reasonably incurred in any case under this paragraph in which the complainant has substantially prevailed.

(3)(A) In any suit brought under the provisions of subsection (g)(1)(B) of this section, the court may enjoin the agency from withholding the records and order the production to the complainant of any agency records improperly withheld from him. In such a case the court shall determine the matter de novo, and may examine the contents of any agency records in camera to determine whether the records or any portion thereof may be withheld under any of the exemptions set forth in subsection (k) of this section, and the burden is on the agency to sustain its action.

(B) The court may assess against the United States reasonable attorney fees and other litigation costs reasonably incurred in any case under this paragraph in which the complainant has substantially prevailed.

(4) In any suit brought under the provisions of subsection (g) (1)(C) or (D) of this section in which the court determines that the agency acted in a manner which was intentional or willful, the United States shall be liable to the individual in an amount equal to the sum of--

(A) actual damages sustained by the individual as a result of the refusal or failure, but in no case shall a person entitled to recovery receive less than the sum of $1,000; and

(B) the costs of the action together with reasonable attorney fees as determined by the court.

(5) An action to enforce any liability created under this section may be brought in the district court of the United States in the district in which the complainant resides, or has his principal place of business, or in which the agency records are situated, or in the District of Columbia, without regard to the amount in controversy, within two years from the date on which the cause of action arises, except that where an agency has materially and willfully misrepresented any information required under this section to be disclosed to an individual and the information so misrepresented is material to establishment of the liability of the agency to the individual under this section, the action may be brought at any time within two years after discovery by the individual of the misrepresentation. Nothing in this section shall be construed to authorize any civil action by reason of any injury sustained as the result of a disclosure of a record prior to September 27, 1975.

(h) Rights of legal guardians.

For the purposes of this section, the parent of any minor, or the legal guardian of any individual who has been declared to be incompetent due to physical or mental incapacity or age by a court of competent jurisdiction, may act on behalf of the individual.

(i)(1) Criminal penalties.

Any officer or employee of an agency, who by virtue of his employment or official position, has possession of, or access to, agency records which contain individually identifiable information the disclosure of which is prohibited by this section or by rules or regulations established thereunder, and who knowing that disclosure of the specific material is so prohibited, willfully discloses the material in any manner to any person or agency not entitled to receive it, shall be guilty of a misdemeanor and fined not more than $5,000.

> (2) Any officer or employee of any agency who willfully maintains a system of records without meeting the notice requirements of subsection (e)(4) of this section shall be guilty of a misdemeanor and fined not more than $5,000.

> (3) Any person who knowingly and willfully requests or obtains any record concerning an individual from an agency under false pretenses shall be guilty of a misdemeanor and fined not more than $5,000.

(j) General exemptions.

The head of any agency may promulgate rules, in accordance with the requirements (including general notice) of sections 553(b)(1), (2), and (3), (c), and (e) of this title, to exempt any system of records within the agency from any part of this section except subsections (b), (c)(1) and (2), (e)(4)(A) through (F), (e)(6), (7), (9), (10), and (11), and (i) if the system of records is--

(1) maintained by the Central Intelligence Agency; or

(2) maintained by an agency or component thereof which performs as its principal function any activity pertaining to the enforcement of criminal laws, including police efforts to prevent, control, or reduce crime or to apprehend criminals, and the activities of prosecutors, courts, correctional, probation, pardon, or parole authorities, and which consists of (A) information compiled for the purpose of identifying individual criminal offenders and alleged offenders and consisting only of identifying data and notations of arrests, the nature and disposition of criminal charges, sentencing, confinement, release, and parole and probation status; (B) information compiled for the purpose of a criminal investigation, including reports of informants and investigators, and associated with an identifiable individual; or (C) reports identifiable to an individual compiled at any stage of the process of enforcement of the criminal laws from arrest or indictment through release from supervision.

At the time rules are adopted under this subsection, the agency shall include in the statement required under section 553(c) of this title, the reasons why the system of records is to be exempted from a provision of this section.

(k) Specific exemptions.

The head of any agency may promulgate rules, in accordance with the requirements (including general notice) of sections 553(b)(1), (2), and (3), (c), and (e) of this title, to exempt any system of records within the agency from subsections (c)(3), (d), (e)(1), (e)(4)(G), (H), and (I) and (f) of this section if the system of records is--

(1) subject to the provisions of section 552(b)(1) of this title;

(2) investigatory material compiled for law enforcement purposes, other than material within the scope of subsection (j)(2) of this section: Provided, however, That if any individual is denied any right, privilege, or benefit that he would otherwise be entitled by Federal law, or for which he would otherwise be eligible, as a result of the maintenance of such material, such material shall be provided to such individual, except to the extent that the disclosure of such material would reveal the identity of a source who furnished information to the Government under an express promise that the identity of the source would be held in confidence, or, prior to the effective date of this section, under an implied promise that the identity of the source would be held in confidence;

(3) maintained in connection with providing protective services to the President of the United States or other individuals pursuant to section 3056 of title 18;

(4) required by statute to be maintained and used solely as statistical records;

(5) investigatory material compiled solely for the purpose of determining suitability, eligibility, or qualifications for Federal civilian employment, military service, Federal contracts, or access to classified information, but only to the extent that the disclosure of such material would reveal the identity of a source who furnished information to the Government under an express promise that the identity of the source would be held in confidence, or, prior to the effective date of this section, under an implied promise that the identity of the source would be held in confidence;

(6) testing or examination material used solely to determine individual qualifications for appointment or promotion in the Federal service the disclosure of which would compromise the objectivity or fairness of the testing or examination process; or

(7) evaluation material used to determine potential for promotion in the armed services, but only to the extent that the disclosure of such material would reveal the identity of a source who furnished information to the Government under an express promise that the identity of the source would be held in confidence, or, prior to the effective date of this section, under an implied promise that the identity of the source would be held in confidence.

At the time rules are adopted under this subsection, the agency shall include in the statement required under section 553(c) of this title, the reasons why the system of records is to be exempted from a provision of this section.

(l)(1) Archival records.

Each agency record which is accepted by the Archivist of the United States for storage, processing, and servicing in accordance with section 3103 of title 44 shall, for the purposes of this section, be considered to be maintained by the agency which deposited the record and shall be subject to the provisions of this section. The Archivist of the United States shall not disclose the record except to the agency which maintains the record, or under rules established by that agency which are not inconsistent with the provisions of this section.

(2) Each agency record pertaining to an identifiable individual which was transferred to the National Archives of the United States as a record which has sufficient historical

or other value to warrant its continued preservation by the United States Government, prior to the effective date of this section, shall, for the purposes of this section, be considered to be maintained by the National Archives and shall not be subject to the provisions of this section, except that a statement generally describing such records (modeled after the requirements relating to records subject to subsections (e)(4)(A) through (G) of this section) shall be published in the Federal Register.

(3) Each agency record pertaining to an identifiable individual which is transferred to the National Archives of the United States as a record which has sufficient historical or other value to warrant its continued preservation by the United States Government, on or after the effective date of this section, shall, for the purposes of this section, be considered to be maintained by the National Archives and shall be exempt from the requirements of this section except subsections (e)(4)(A) through (G) and (e)(9) of this section.

(m)(1) Government contractors.

When an agency provides by a contract for the operation by or on behalf of the agency of a system of records to accomplish an agency function, the agency shall, consistent with its authority, cause the requirements of this section to be applied to such system. For purposes of subsection (i) of this section any such contractor and any employee of such contractor, if such contract is agreed to on or after the effective date of this section, shall be considered to be an employee of an agency.

(2) A consumer reporting agency to which a record is disclosed under section 3711(e) of title 31 shall not be considered a contractor for the purposes of this section.

(n) Mailing lists.

An individual's name and address may not be sold or rented by an agency unless such action is specifically authorized by law. This provision shall not be construed to require the withholding of names and addresses otherwise permitted to be made public.

(o) Matching agreements.

(1) No record which is contained in a system of records may be disclosed to a recipient agency or non-Federal agency for use in a computer matching program except pursuant to a written agreement between the source agency and the recipient agency or non-Federal agency specifying--

(A) the purpose and legal authority for conducting the program;

(B) the justification for the program and the anticipated results, including a specific estimate of any savings;

(C) a description of the records that will be matched, including each data element that will be used, the approximate number of records that will be matched, and the projected starting and completion dates of the matching program;

(D) procedures for providing individualized notice at the time of application, and notice periodically thereafter as directed by the Data Integrity Board of such agency (subject to guidance provided by the Director of the Office of Management and Budget pursuant to subsection (v)), to--

(i) applicants for and recipients of financial assistance or payments under Federal benefit programs, and

(ii) applicants for and holders of positions as Federal personnel, that any information provided by such applicants, recipients, holders, and individuals may be subject to verification through matching programs;

(E) procedures for verifying information produced in such matching program as required by subsection (p);

(F) procedures for the retention and timely destruction of identifiable records created by a recipient agency or non-Federal agency in such matching program;

(G) procedures for ensuring the administrative, technical, and physical security of the records matched and the results of such programs;

(H) prohibitions on duplication and redisclosure of records provided by the source agency within or outside the recipient agency or the non-Federal agency, except where required by law or essential to the conduct of the matching program;

(I) procedures governing the use by a recipient agency or non-Federal agency of records provided in a matching program by a source agency, including procedures governing return of the records to the source agency or destruction of records used in such program;

(J) information on assessments that have been made on the accuracy of the records that will be used in such matching program; and

(K) that the Comptroller General may have access to all records of a recipient agency or a non-Federal agency that the Comptroller General deems necessary in order to monitor or verify compliance with the agreement.

(2)(A) A copy of each agreement entered into pursuant to paragraph (1) shall--

(i) be transmitted to the Committee on Governmental Affairs of the Senate and the Committee on Government Operations of the House of Representatives; and

(ii) be available upon request to the public.

(B) No such agreement shall be effective until 30 days after the date on which such a copy is transmitted pursuant to subparagraph (A)(i).

(C) Such an agreement shall remain in effect only for such period, not to exceed 18 months, as the Data Integrity Board of the agency determines is appropriate in light of the purposes, and length of time necessary for the conduct, of the matching program.

(D) Within 3 months prior to the expiration of such an agreement pursuant to subparagraph (C), the Data Integrity Board of the agency may, without additional review, renew the matching agreement for a current, ongoing matching program for not more than one additional year if--

(i) such program will be conducted without any change; and

(ii) each party to the agreement certifies to the Board in writing that the program has been conducted in compliance with the agreement.

(p) Verification and opportunity to contest findings.

(1) In order to protect any individual whose records are used in a matching program, no recipient agency, non-Federal agency, or source agency may suspend, terminate, reduce, or make a final denial of any financial assistance or payment under a Federal benefit program to such individual, or take other adverse action against such individual, as a result of information produced by such matching program, until--

(A)(i) the agency has independently verified the information; or

(ii) the Data Integrity Board of the agency, or in the case of a non-Federal agency the Data Integrity Board of the source agency, determines in accordance with guidance issued by the Director of the Office of Management and Budget that--

(I) the information is limited to identification and amount of benefits paid by the source agency under a Federal benefit program; and

(II) there is a high degree of confidence that the information provided to the recipient agency is accurate;

(B) the individual receives a notice from the agency containing a statement of its findings and informing the individual of the opportunity to contest such findings; and

(C)(i) the expiration of any time period established for the program by statute or regulation for the individual to respond to that notice; or

(ii) in the case of a program for which no such period is established, the end of the 30-day period beginning on the date on which notice under subparagraph (B) is mailed or otherwise provided to the individual.

(2) Independent verification referred to in paragraph (1) requires investigation and confirmation of specific information relating to an individual that is used as a basis for an adverse action against the individual, including where applicable investigation and confirmation of--

(A) the amount of any asset or income involved;

(B) whether such individual actually has or had access to such asset or income for such individual's own use; and

(C) the period or periods when the individual actually had such asset or income.

(3) Notwithstanding paragraph (1), an agency may take any appropriate action otherwise prohibited by such paragraph if the agency determines that the public health or public safety may be adversely affected or significantly threatened during any notice period required by such paragraph.

(q) Sanctions.

(1) Notwithstanding any other provision of law, no source agency may disclose any record which is contained in a system of records to a recipient agency or non-Federal agency for a matching program if such source agency has reason to believe that the requirements of subsection (p), or any matching agreement entered into pursuant to subsection (o), or both, are not being met by such recipient agency.

(2) No source agency may renew a matching agreement unless--

(A) the recipient agency or non-Federal agency has certified that it has complied with the provisions of that agreement; and

(B) the source agency has no reason to believe that the certification is inaccurate.

(r) Report on new systems and matching programs.

Each agency that proposes to establish or make a significant change in a system of records or a matching program shall provide adequate advance notice of any such proposal (in duplicate) to the Committee on Government Operations of the House of Representatives, the Committee on Governmental Affairs of the Senate, and the Office of Management and Budget in order to permit an evaluation of the probable or potential effect of such proposal on the privacy or other rights of individuals.

(s) Biennial report.

The President shall biennially submit to the Speaker of the House of Representatives and the President pro tempore of the Senate a report--

(1) describing the actions of the Director of the Office of Management and Budget pursuant to section 6 of the Privacy Act of 1974 during the preceding 2 years;

(2) describing the exercise of individual rights of access and amendment under this section during such years;

(3) identifying changes in or additions to systems of records;

(4) containing such other information concerning administration of this section as may be necessary or useful to the Congress in reviewing the effectiveness of this section in carrying out the purposes of the Privacy Act of 1974.

(t)(1) Effect of other laws.

No agency shall rely on any exemption contained in section 552 of this title to withhold from an individual any record which is otherwise accessible to such individual under the provisions of this section.

(2) No agency shall rely on any exemption in this section to withhold from an individual any record which is otherwise accessible to such individual under the provisions of section 552 of this title.

(u) Data Integrity Boards.

(1) Every agency conducting or participating in a matching program shall establish a Data Integrity Board to oversee and coordinate among the various components of such agency the agency's implementation of this section.

(2) Each Data Integrity Board shall consist of senior officials designated by the head of the agency, and shall include any senior official designated by the head of the agency as responsible for implementation of this section, and the inspector general of the agency, if any. The inspector general shall not serve as chairman of the Data Integrity Board.

(3) Each Data Integrity Board--

(A) shall review, approve, and maintain all written agreements for receipt or disclosure of agency records for matching programs to ensure compliance with subsection (o), and all relevant statutes, regulations, and guidelines;

(B) shall review all matching programs in which the agency has participated during the year, either as a source agency or recipient agency, determine compliance with applicable laws, regulations, guidelines, and agency agreements, and assess the costs and benefits of such programs;

(C) shall review all recurring matching programs in which the agency has participated during the year, either as a source agency or recipient agency, for continued justification for such disclosures;

(D) shall compile an annual report, which shall be submitted to the head of the agency and the Office of Management and Budget and made available to the public on request, describing the matching activities of the agency, including--

(i) matching programs in which the agency has participated as a source agency or recipient agency;

(ii) matching agreements proposed under subsection (o) that were disapproved by the Board;

(iii) any changes in membership or structure of the Board in the preceding year;

(iv) the reasons for any waiver of the requirement in paragraph (4) of this section for completion and submission of a cost-benefit analysis prior to the approval of a matching program;

(v) any violations of matching agreements that have been alleged or identified and any corrective action taken; and

(vi) any other information required by the Director of the Office of Management and Budget to be included in such report;

(E) shall serve as a clearinghouse for receiving and providing information on the accuracy, completeness, and reliability of records used in matching programs;

(F) shall provide interpretation and guidance to agency components and personnel on the requirements of this section for matching programs;

(G) shall review agency recordkeeping and disposal policies and practices for matching programs to assure compliance with this section; and

(H) may review and report on any agency matching activities that are not matching programs.

(4)(A) Except as provided in subparagraphs (B) and (C), a Data Integrity Board shall not approve any written agreement for a matching program unless the agency has completed and submitted to such Board a cost-benefit analysis of the proposed program and such analysis demonstrates that the program is likely to be cost effective.

(B) The Board may waive the requirements of subparagraph (A) of this paragraph if it determines in writing, in accordance with guidelines prescribed by the Director of the Office of Management and Budget, that a cost-benefit analysis is not required.

(C) A cost-benefit analysis shall not be required under subparagraph (A) prior to the initial approval of a written agreement for a matching program that is specifically required by statute. Any subsequent written agreement for such a program shall not be approved by the Data Integrity Board unless the agency has submitted a cost-benefit analysis of the program as conducted under the preceding approval of such agreement.

(5)(A) If a matching agreement is disapproved by a Data Integrity Board, any party to such agreement may appeal the disapproval to the Director of the Office of Management and Budget. Timely notice of the filing of such an appeal shall be provided by the Director of the Office of Management and Budget to the Committee on Governmental Affairs of the Senate and the Committee on Government Operations of the House of Representatives.

(B) The Director of the Office of Management and Budget may approve a matching agreement notwithstanding the disapproval of a Data Integrity Board if the Director determines that--

(i) the matching program will be consistent with all applicable legal, regulatory, and policy requirements;

(ii) there is adequate evidence that the matching agreement will be cost-effective; and

(iii) the matching program is in the public interest.

(C) The decision of the Director to approve a matching agreement shall not take effect until 30 days after it is reported to committees described in subparagraph (A).

(D) If the Data Integrity Board and the Director of the Office of Management and Budget disapprove a matching program proposed by the inspector general of an agency, the inspector general may report the disapproval to the head of the agency and to the Congress.

(6) In the reports required by paragraph (3)(D), agency matching activities that are not matching programs may be reported on an aggregate basis, if and to the extent necessary to protect ongoing law enforcement or counterintelligence investigations.

(v) Office of Management and Budget responsibilities.

The Director of the Office of Management and Budget shall--

(1) develop and, after notice and opportunity for public comment, prescribe guidelines and regulations for the use of agencies in implementing the provisions of this section; and

(2) provide continuing assistance to and oversight of the implementation of this section by agencies.

Archives.gov Home Contact Us Privacy Policy Accessibility
Freedom of Information Act No FEAR Act Top of Page
http://www.archives.gov/about/laws/privacy-act-1974.html

END OF THE BOOK

ABOUT THE AUTHOR

Harry Katzan, Jr. is a professor who has written several books and peer-reviewed technical papers on computers and related subjcts. He wrote one of the first books on computer security and cloud computing, perhaps the first on these interesting subjects. He has been a consultant on computer security and artificial intelligence and has taught cybersecurity in the graduate level at a large university. He and his wife have lived in Switzerland where he was an executive consultant and a visiting professor. He holds bachelors, masters, and doctorate degrees.

BOOKS BY HARRY KATZAN JR

COMPUTERS AND INFORMATION SYSTEMS

Advanced Programming
APL Programming and Computer Techniques
APL Users Guide
Computer Organization and the System/370
A PL/I Approach to Programming Languages
Introduction to Programming Languages
Operating Systems
Information Technology
Computer Data Security
Introduction to Computer Science
Computer Systems Organization and Programming
Computer Data Management and Database Technology
Systems Design and Documentation
Microprogramming Primer
The IBM 5100 Portable Computer
Fortran 77
The Standard Data Encryption Algorithm
Introduction to Distributed Data Processing
Distributed Information Systems
Invitation to Pascal
Invitation to Forth
Microcomputer Graphics and Programming Techniques
Invitation to Ada
Invitation to Ada and Ada Reference Manual
Invitation to Mapper
Operating Systems (2nd Edition)
Local Area Networks
Invitation to MVS (with D. Tharayil)
Privacy, Identity, and Cloud Computing

BUSINESS AND MANAGEMENT

Multinational Computer Systems
Office Automation
Management Support Systems
A Manager's Guide to Productivity, Quality
Circles, and Industrial Robots
Quality Circle Management
Service and Advanced Technology

RESEARCH

Managing Uncertainty

SERVICE SCIENCE

A Manager's Guide to Service Science
Foundations of Service Science
Service Science
Introduction to Service
Service Concepts for Management
A Collection of Service Essays
Hospitality and Service

NOVELS
The Matt and the General Series

The Mysterious Case of the Royal Baby
The Curious Case of the Royal Marriage
The Auspicious Case of the General and the Royal Family
A Case of Espionage
Shelter in Place
The Virus
The Pandemic

Life is Good
The Vaccine
A Tale of Discovery
The Terrorist Plot
An Untimely Situation

LITTLE BOOKS

The Little Book of Artificial Intelligence
The Little Book of System Management
The Little Book of Cybersecurity
The Little Book of Cloud Computing

*****

Printed in the United States
by Baker & Taylor Publisher Services